A BRIDGE TO SPIRIT

A Bridge to Spirit

Understanding Conscious Self Development and Consciousness-Altering Substances

LISA ROMERO

INNERWORK BOOKS | 2019

2019

INNERWORK BOOKS

PO Box 1064
Mullumbimby NSW 2482
Australia

ISBN: 978-0-6485789-2-5 (paperback)
ISBN: 978-0-6484904-1-8 (ebook)

Contents

This book was written in gratitude to my
Developing the Self – Developing the World
colleagues, who dedicate their time to bringing
this work in the form of individual health and wellbeing
programs and student, parent, and teacher education
in order to support community wellbeing.

To find support for further education or for transforming
the effects of substance use,
see our program at <u>developingtheself.org</u>.

Introduction

AT DIFFERENT STAGES of humanity's development, it often appears that a leap forward in our progression is necessary. And although in recent history this call for progression has been articulated many times by different traditions of the inner schooling path, it appears that a quickening of the changes in the outer world is demanding a more imminent shift. It seems that today we are all preparing for a change in consciousness that, in turn, needs to change the way the outer world progresses. The awareness of the environmental damage from our external industrialized existence is also alerting people more intensively to the need for inner change as we become increasingly aware of the effects of outer imbalances upon the interior life of human beings.

If you are a part of the 60% of people whose lives have outwardly improved as a result of the industrial revolution, then it is hard to complain about the errors that the industrialized world has inflicted upon our outer lives. However, as a result of this outer industrialization, our inner lives are suffering. In one sense, many people enjoy more materialistically abundant lives in today's industrialized world than had ever been possible in the past, and yet the materialistic world is not satisfying the interior life of many human beings. We have at our fingertips everything that we need to stimulate our senses, to gratify our needs, and yet we continue to progress into conditions of greater depression, greater anxiety, and the restless recognition that we are not fulfilled by the growing materialism that has promised to satisfy us.

Reports indicate growing states of isolation; and as each year progresses, more people are claiming to experience deep states of loneliness. Mental illnesses are consistently on the rise, with an incredible increase in individuals who need anti-depressants, anti-anxiety medications, and mood stabilizers. We have more support outwardly, but we have less support inwardly. We are beginning to see that the interior world of our thinking, feeling, and willing is also being affected. We have become interiorly industrialized human beings, and this is not healthy for our interior world.

Those who seek the spirit are aware, on some level, that we stand in need of greater health and wellbeing for the interior life of humankind and that this health can be found in spiritual practices. A spiritual life helps us to grow beyond our limited self-experience; it is a form of nourishment that comes from beyond the realm of sensory input, even though it may be evoked by the external wonders of the natural world. This spiritual life awakens in our interior life and can be developed and nurtured through building a relationship to the divine spiritual world.

It has long been taught that inner development, meditation, and contemplation lead, for those who devote time to their cultivation, to inner peace, resilience, and strength;

and so we could expect that in our age more and more individuals would look to internal practices as a way of strengthening their inner system of support and countering the agitation and emptiness created by our increasingly disconnected and materialistic external life. However, even with this emerging internal need, we are not seeing a proliferation of these traditional paths of development. It is thought that financial and material security have turned many people away from the inner path provided by a religious life and faith – the paths along which many have gained inner resilience in the past. Some even think that it is on account of our level of material security itself that we have seen the demise of organized religion in our age.

That being said, individuals still seek spiritual practices of inner development for the purpose of achieving greater wellbeing. The scientific recognition of the effectiveness of certain practices has resulted in their incorporation into daily life in order to help reduce stress. We have seen, for instance, that mindfulness meditation has been taken up widely by many individuals to help manage life. Mindfulness is being used by corporations to foster wellbeing in the workplace, and has even been taught in the Houses of Parliament. It is being utilized in a mainstream way to support an interior life that now requires focused attention in order to find the inner stability and certainty that, for many, were once a natural endowment.

It is important to note that in the past, meditation was never given as a counterforce to help us to manage our outer lives. Never before in human history has meditation been used as a medication, remedy, or therapy in the way it is being used today. Today meditation is often sold as a technique to make our everyday life easier, to prevent us from feeling disturbed inwardly, to allow us to center ourselves and calm ourselves down, and to help us to get to sleep at night. Although these may indeed be the natural consequences of meditation in the meditant's daily experience, the essential activity of meditation is to develop the human being's consciousness beyond the sense world into other realms of consciousness.

Meditation, as taught through the various schools, has long been given as the path to enlightenment and illumination or greater unity with the divine, as the path toward bringing illumination to a human being regarding the truth and realities that exist beyond the sense-world experience of self. Meditation has been given so that we may become conscious in the realms of consciousness in which we are otherwise asleep. Inner development and meditation provide the path toward developing the faculties and capacities needed in order for us to have insight and experience in other realms of consciousness.

The devoted path of meditation can appear to be a slow path toward awakening to the experiences of the spirit, especially in light of the instantaneous effects of consciousness-altering substances, which seem to allow an individual to have experiences similar to those generated by the practicing meditant, but do so without requiring the years of training and dedication through which most meditants have had to work.

Why, then, is it necessary to work with practices of inner development if the results can already be found in a plant? Are there benefits to being given experiences of other realms of consciousness by consuming something that produces these effects? Are there benefits to inducing capacities that the individual has not developed by their own effort, but that are rather the result of consuming consciousness-altering substances? What is it that draws people to use substances on the path of inner development today?

By understanding the steps and stages cultivated through interior development, and the corresponding keys that allow us to access doorways leading to other realms of consciousness, we may begin to clarify these questions. This small book begins to explore these questions in a twofold way: 1.) by correlating the meditative experiences with the realms of consciousness that they serve to awaken within, and 2.) by correlating the given effects of various consciousness-altering substances with the doorways that they appear to open.

It is always difficult to present pictures that correspond to every individual's experience, simply because we each walk the path of life and the path to the spirit in a unique way; and yet, there are some definite pillars that we will find we all have in common. For instance, most children crawl before they walk, and there is evidence to suggest that this supports the development of the child. There are definite milestones that the developing child will pass through regardless of the influences of various cultures and different approaches to child-rearing. Certain steps and stages can be found in every human being from birth to adulthood.

Once the body has reached maturity in adulthood, thereby liberating all of the human being's forces from the need to flow into the growth of the physical body, we are ready to take up the path of our inner development. However, this will not necessarily include meditation because not everyone needs to be aware of realms of consciousness that extend beyond our daily consciousness. But if you have found yourself seeking beyond this everyday realm and its realities, whether on account of the need to heal the industrialized interior state or the desire to grow your human capacity, then the path of meditation is one of the primary ways of working in this direction.

Within a particular phase of evolution, the path of opening up to other states of consciousness will involve some structured forms that are common to us all. And then, just as one child may experience a very different upbringing from another, so as individuals we may each have a very distinct "upbringing" in terms of our growing relationship to the spiritual world.

In the rarest of occasions, we hear of a human being that skips developmental stages; for instance, the story of a child born walking. Some say the Buddha was born already able to walk. These stories should not be taken as literal facts, but as pictures characterizing esoteric realities of the advancement of that individuality.

In the primary steps of inner development achieved through meditation and inner practice, and in the realities of the other realms of consciousness that are thereby entered, there are very few differences relating to the culture, race, or community of the one entering this path. It is only our ability to describe those realms, as well as the meaning we give to the symbols or signs within a given teaching, that may vary according to points of view originating in different cultures, societies, streams, or communities. Each of these points of view may provide a different language or interpretation of inner experience. Each may give a different directive as to how we are to enter these realms according to the particular schooling or training in question.

And so it is said that "there are many paths to the top of the mountain, but the view is the same for everyone who makes it to the top." However, it is useful today for each person to understand what is required of us in order to make our way safely to the top, and indeed to understand the very purpose and value of ultimately being able to see the view from that highest point.

Over a relatively short period of time, humanity has undergone a great change in its relationship to the realities of spiritual life. When we look to the ancient traditions, regardless of a particular tradition's religious heritage there has always been a common understanding that there is in fact a world of the spirit. Regardless of the way in which this has been described, there has always been a general recognition of the existence of powers with capacities beyond those of the human being that guide us and work with us. Today, however, atheism is growing like a new religion. There is a belief in the seemingly final conclusions of science, even though science itself is ever-changing. There is a ready belief in any and all empirical science. And when we ask why the sciences are now receiving the sort of blind faith that used to be given to religion even though much scientific research is often done under the influence of money and politics, then we may be able to recognize the depths of change that are taking place in so many individuals' own connections with the spirit in the world.

This change is taking place quite rapidly. Individuals everywhere can feel a disconnect between the outer reality and their inner world of feeling; their feeling life is not engaging, relating to, or connecting with the outer world or the "other" with the same depth as before – it is not connecting in a meaningful way, in a way that moves the feeling life to recognize that there is something beyond the limited physical self.

Numerous people, when looking upon the wonders of nature, can feel removed from these wonders. No joy arises in them at the rising of the sun, no experience of wonder at the vastness of the expansive oceans, no awe at the night sky – only an inner disconnect. Many people today are unmoved by the experiences of the outer world; or, even if they are moved at the moment of experience, it does not have a lasting impact that keeps them inwardly nourished. Our experiencing inner world has become dulled. We are not inwardly stirred enough by life, even by the wonders of the world, to profess the glory of the spirit.

Materialistic thinking has grown stronger in our present age. Like a gatekeeper of the inner life of experience, we allow ourselves to be held back by the academic rigor required of "proof," or in dwelling on the literal meaning of things. Literalism is the new baseline of the thinking life of many of the industrialized peoples. The inner experience of the arts, which could offer health to our inner life, has now become in many cases merely a matter of being clever. Intellectualism is seen as being advanced and of a higher standing in comparison to the non-intellectual disposition.

Our industrialized will now seeks for self-reward. Our industrialized will often works against what is healthy and harmonious in our own body, in our emotions, and in our mind. Many are persuaded to steadily consume – or are even addicted to – unhealthy nourishment entering by mouth or mind in the course of their progression to the grave. Many begin to look upon this earth as something that is becoming empty, an empty grave, and begin to feel that life is about getting as much out of the world as you can before you die – before it dies.

Although we are faced with a world that, for many, is devoid of all spiritual reality, there are still many seekers on the path. The seeker is looking toward the uniting love of the life of spirit, and those who seek the path know that beyond this sense-perceptible world there exists more than meets the eye. They have awakened the inner will toward the light and they will not give up just because it is becoming more difficult to find. We need to strengthen our hearts to be able not only to meet the challenges of what faces us, but to work out of the impulse of love into the future, and out of love to take the next necessary leap forward for humanity's progression.

A Bridge to Spirit: Conscious Inner Development and Consciousness-Altering Substances

WHEN WE BEGIN treading the path of inner development, we are presented with the task of understanding the dimensions of our human experience and experiencing these dimensions for ourselves with greater awareness than we had been capable of before. From the very outset, we are required to expand beyond our own present experience of ourselves. We are both physical and spiritual, and there is a possibility of experiencing the truth of this fact and participating in the realities of "the heavens and the earth" with full consciousness, if we have the will to do so.

The modern path of self-development works with these aspects of our humanness. On one hand, the individuality that utilizes the physical body, emotional or psyche body, and mental body, is worked upon in order that it may gain separation from its own subjective, personalized experience and thereby enter into relationship with the more objective human faculties with which every human being is endowed. On the other hand, we work to awaken a relationship to our spiritual nature and to the experiences that arise through our evolving connection to the spiritual world. In working with this apparent duality, a new activity – a third reality – comes into being. This third reality is the bridge that we build between the two worlds in which we participate: the physical and spiritual worlds.

There is a difference between inner development, or self-development, and meditation. Many individuals will walk upon the path of self-development without ever taking up a meditative practice, while today there are also others who engage in a meditative practice without incorporating self-development. There are many different techniques for learning to climb the mountain of self-transformation, but most paths that bear transformative results bring with them certain attainments that are common to all who walk the path. Most traditions have different names for these steps that are to be surmounted, but regardless of the schooling path we choose to utilize, there are some processes common to all paths that lead to growth. These processes can be identified, and they are different from the experience of the inner capacities with which we started our inner development path.

Today, meditation is often given as a counterforce to the stress of everyday life. It is taken up by individuals with the aim of managing the intensity of life so that they may find peace in the midst of turbulence, strength in the midst of chaos. This in itself is a new phenomenon. In the past, meditation was never given to counteract the effects of sensory existence and the difficulties we face within it. Meditation's purpose has always been to bring the individual into a conscious relationship to realms of being of which we are otherwise unconscious. And many in our modern age have mixed together their understanding of the meditative path and the self-development path.

Self-development allows us to distinguish the *personal* conditioning and content of our inner world from the *external* indoctrination, education, and conditioning that has come through family, culture, religion, beliefs, and so forth. It also allows us to bring order to the threefold nature of our inner world: the content of our thinking or our mental body, our feeling body containing all our emotions, and our will impulses and habits. And in organizing the content of our inner world, we can begin to recognize that our *faculties of perception* are not one and the same as the *content* that we perceive by means of them. We learn, with greater and more persistent clarity, to separate the content of our inner world from the faculties and capacities within us.

Between the world of the sensory earthly life and the world of the spirit, the human being treading the path of self-development and meditation now creates the bridge that unites the experiences arising from the physical and spiritual life. These aspects of self in many ways remain separate in the consciousness of the industrialized individual's inner life and, in our age, we tend to automatically orient ourselves toward the self of the earthly personality. However, we are not entirely cut off from the possibility of knowing and experiencing our spiritual being and the spiritual realities. The physical, emotional, and mental faculties that exist within our everyday experience contain within them the building blocks needed to bridge what at first appears to be the duality of the physical and the spiritual, back into a unity, if the human being freely chooses to do so.

In self-development, the individual works upon the content of their own personal inner life, and in doing so gains awareness of the faculties that are not personal but common to all human beings. The vast majority of our thinking is a matter of the heritage into which we are conditioned, indoctrinated, or educated. But our *faculty to think* is a human capacity that each of us has. To begin with, the personality is identified primarily with the content of thinking and not with the capacity to think or the faculty of thinking. But by ordering and assessing the content of our own thought life, by being self-directed and through self-evaluation, the experience begins to arise that my thoughts that have been handed down to me or educated within me are like items cluttering up a room in my head. As I order and organize these items – some being antiques passed through generations and some belonging to me simply because I have been born in a particular place or culture – I become aware of the room in which they exist. This room arises into consciousness through what is sometimes called the "witness" or the "observer" within.

The observer or witness is awakened through self-development by the activity of concentrating our thinking and self-assessing, and in this way being able to bear witness, or observe, the experiences taking place within us. On the path of self-development, this observer awakens, or becomes active, only when we activate it. It is not a natural state. The natural state is to be identified with the content of our thinking. It is an important step in self-development to move from the content of our thinking to an awareness of the room within which thinking is perceived as being active.

Self-development also works on the emotional or feeling content of the personality. Our feeling life or emotions have also been developed through certain social or cultural beliefs. For instance, we express grief very differently from one culture to another. If we are born into a society that worships the moon, then when seeing the moon we would have a certain feeling-experience on account of the conditions that have educated us to feel a particular way about it. This is a conditioned feeling-response. We can be conditioned to feel certain ways about other countries, other peoples, or the things of the world. Of course, this is a process involving a combination of our thinking and feeling, but part of the self-development path involves an attempt to distinguish between the thinking processes, feeling processes, and will impulses that work as a unity in the personality, interacting with and triggering each other. Through the inner development path, an essential bridge toward spiritual experiences is found in the capacity to move from the *content* of our feeling life to the *capacity* to feel or to have an "experiencing interior" that allows for objective feelings as opposed to merely subjective and personal ones.

The third self-development process that needs to be taken hold of is in some ways the hardest, as it amounts to taking hold of our will impulses. Many of our unconscious impulses are very deeply bound to our bodily chemistry and to the pathways that have been etched into us throughout our development. We have the habits of our bodies, which are habits of will, and those habits in turn affect our feeling and our thinking because our mental, emotional, and physical processes work as a unity in the personality even though they may indeed battle against each other.

Because the will is bound to the body, there may be bodily impulses, such as the sexual drive, that contradict the indoctrination or the education of our thinking about sexuality. And our thinking may affect our feeling, causing us to feel shame; or our will impulses may affect our feeling, causing us to feel desire. Although these work as a unity and react upon each other, they can also be in conflict – and the conflict is inevitably a matter of an impulse from within that fights against the conditioning from without.

This inner conflict between our education, our feeling experience, and our will or bodily impulses can be the instigator for why an individual may choose self-development. What arises as a discord internally between thinking, feeling, and will impulses may arise not only because one conditioning stands against another as an inner contradiction, but because our individualized free will, which is not our conditioned will, begins to awaken as a "will striving toward the divine."

On the self-development path, the free individualized will requires strengthening. This free will is not bound to conditioning, and each human being has this seed of freedom. Strengthening the free individualized will can be achieved in various ways. We can use the instrument of our own inner world and apply our will to our thinking. This not only supports the ordering of our thoughts but also strengthens our free individualized will, because much of our will is simply not free but rather pulled upon by bodily impulses and conditioned patterns that have created habits of will. We can also bring our will into our feeling. If we take the following exercise of the rising sun and the rising moon, we can recognize that the free will is one of the most important capacities in our self-development path.

Close your eyes and imagine the rising sun. Don't just *see* it – which is bringing your will into your thinking – but also *feel* it, which is bringing your will into your feeling. You're not trying to pull upon a memory of the rising sun you once saw, but in the present moment you are activating the rising sun that you can cultivate right now.

By being a participant in earthly life, you have at some point seen the rising sun, and you have experienced it to one degree or another depending on the clarity of your capacity of interior experiencing. But now, with the will, we can rebuild within us the thought-imagination of the rising sun and the experience of the rising sun. This develops a strength in our will through the fact that we are internally taking hold of our thinking and our feeling to a much greater degree than would be the case if we were merely to direct our attention outwardly to the rising sun. This is because in the sense world the outer thing that draws our attention provides, through its very presence, at least 50% of the will's engagement. Our freedom lies in maintaining our attention in the direction that we choose. But in the inner world, if it falls upon me to cultivate the image and the feeling, then I have to engage far more will activity out of myself.

We can now strengthen this further by turning to inwardly cultivating the rising moon in the dark night's sky. And we can recognize that if I inwardly cultivate the picture of the rising moon and I inwardly experience the differences that this brings, through my will, into my feeling, then I can also experience how these different cosmic bodies bring different qualities to the world both outside of me and inside of me.

If we wish to explore the external world, then internalizing those outer things and inwardly thinking and feeling them not only strengthens our free will, but it also separates them from the impression they make on our senses and instead builds for us an internal impression of these processes. As a part of human inner development, this has a deep effect on strengthening our individualized free will. This strengthening is needed in order to think and experience the inner reality of things that do not have an outer manifestation in the sense world. This strengthened will can then take thoughts or insights that stream from the spiritual schooling and think these thoughts, even though we cannot see an external expression of them in the sense world.

In this way, I can engage with purely spiritual truths and experiences without requiring the sense world to prove them to me or present them to me.

Therefore, realities and laws that exist within the realm of spirit, and that cannot be perceived as manifest in the external sense world, can be accessed only by my inner development. For example, the spiritual statement "wisdom lives in the light" first has to be awakened as a reality inwardly before we can perceive that this spiritual reality is also at work within the sense world. On the other hand, we could expand our concepts of the different worlds by picturing that behind the material world is a spiritual counterpart or archetype of which the sensory appearance is only one manifestation. The concept "triangle" exists as a pure archetype, but the triangles I see are manifestations that abide by the laws of being a triangle, or of "triangle-ness."

Inner development not only allows us to have a relationship to the realities residing in the spiritual world, but ultimately deepens our perception of the spiritual world within the sense world.

Once again, the potential for humanity to develop clarified faculties, which can only be developed through life on earth, is the bridge we now need to build between the heavens and the earth. The refined human instrument can only be active in this way when our free will actively engages it inwardly. Our inner work consists of the free individualized will working upon the esoteric thought and the experience of this thought that we bring into being in the present moment. In this way, we can become researchers of esoteric truths, laws, and realities.

The free individualized will is our path to liberation from our bondage to the separated state of existence born of materialism, as well as from its concepts of separation that have dominated the human outlook on how the world should progress. It awakens us to a shared world of spiritual truth that unifies our collective striving and surpasses the limited concepts born of separation.

We start by finding a connection to the spiritual processes behind the external appearance of the sense world, but we can then find a connection to spiritual processes that do not appear to be manifested in the sense world at all on account of the fact that our materialistic view has placed a veil over them. From here, we deepen our relationship to these truths, which we first uncover by spiritual means, and find that they are indeed living in the sense world if only we build a bridge to them.

Moving beyond the personality, we find our humanity in the faculties of the observer, the experiencing interior realm, and the free individualized will. All human beings possess the possibility of building this bridge. The observer opens the door to spiritual thought. Through the experiencing interior, the door is opened to experiences of spiritual realties. With the free individualized will, the human being is opened to greater spiritual capacity, a capacity to self-direct in alignment with the spirit in the world and to create with more ability, power, and potential because of the unity with spiritual strength. It is in the activity of our free will that the spiritual strength arising from the beings of the spiritual world unites with us, so that one can be a more useful and potent agent in the surrounding world.

In esoteric schooling, the development from the personality – the subjective, personal self – toward our common humanity – the three faculties of observer, experiencing interior, and free will – is the result of the inner work. The process of awakening the three faculties that the personal self usually fills with its particular content is understood as the "moon" development. Through various practices, we attempt to take everything that has been given from the past, from heredity, and through concentration and a certain self-control and self-reliance we clarify the difference between the content and the faculty. This is a result of most methods of inner development, even if we are not necessarily instructed to know this about them. This development brings us into a greater ability to be in the present moment. This moon awakening sets the ground for the consciously experienced "sun," or spiritual, awakening.

To be fully conscious of our relationship to the spiritual realities requires the moon awakening. The requisite step, therefore, is to begin working on the development of all three of these capacities equally. This will form the bridge. This bridge is essential, as it works in all directions. It allows us to access the spiritual realities and allows us to integrate and bring spiritual revelations into the earthly world. Again, the bridge is developed out of the heritage of the past, but it will also allow us to bring into the world a new future, a future formed according to the divine spiritual realities. If one were to develop just one faculty fully – either the observer, the experiencing interior, or the free will – without developing the others equally and in harmony, then the personality will generally tend toward utilizing the bridge for personal self-gain and selfish means, going against the very purpose of the spiritual sun path.

Ideally, the seeker today, through their own self-assessment, will determine which of these capacities are weaker and which are stronger within them. This is where honest self-appraisal is necessary. Unfortunately, the personality, which needs to defend itself and its existence, almost always overestimates its capacities. But, nevertheless, we can still become aware of these three faculties and evaluate which elements of their activities are in our governance.

The observer can be developed through ordering the content of our own thinking. But the observer can also be developed by utilizing not only the mental but also the emotional and physical bodies. By being able to look upon ourselves as though we were viewing a friend, to look upon our inner world while we are being moved by certain experiences, also strengthens this observer through the observation of the feeling life. Being able to look upon our physicality, observing the rising and falling of the breath, observing sensations within the body, strengthens the observer by utilizing the body, which is the ground of the will. We can see how mindfulness exercises help us to develop the observer.

Each time we wish to engage the observer, we have to do something. We have to enter into the present moment and apply our attention to the subject we are attending to. We have to utilize the seed of our free will in order to bring our attention to whatever we are wishing to observe. This activity raises us from the automatic nature of the personality, in which the majority of people live continuously, to the self-willed state that human beings alone can access. The animal nature can only live within the stream of the automatic, but the human being can raise themselves out of the automatic state, and in doing so, find their humanity through a faculty that belongs to every human being.

Once we have built up the capacity of the observer, this observer self can be accessed fairly quickly just by doing a simple exercise such as the following:

Is This I?

When we work inwardly, we close our eyes so that the senses don't distract us; but if you can meditate with your eyes open, then you can also work while leaving them open. What we are trying to do is to move away from the content of thought and toward the capacity of thought – which is the observer. We use an exercise to engage the observer. If you have done it before, be aware that you can't engage the observer without the will. They are not separate from each other. Normally, the will is partly "given to you" without your activity because of what you are observing. It is not an independent inner free will, but it is actually given "oomph" by the fact that you have something to observe.

Experiencing the pressure of the chair against your body, ask yourself inwardly, "Is this I?" This question is not meant to be answered, but is an assistance that helps us to bring our attention to the thing; by directing our attention in this way, the observer becomes more clarified in contrast to the self that I can look upon. By moving toward the observer and experiencing it, we are trying to induce the observer-force more strongly. Take a moment with each of these experiences before moving on to the next.

Observing the rising and falling of the breath, ask yourself inwardly, "Is this I?"

Becoming aware of any sensations in the body, ask yourself inwardly, "Is this I?" Watch your consciousness as you move it to this next step.

Become aware of the sounds in the space around you and outside. Ask yourself inwardly, "Is this I?"

Being aware of the warmth of the body, ask yourself inwardly, "Is this I?"

Look inward as an observer, asking if anything takes you away from being able to do that, and then bring your attention to it and ask, "Is this I?" This should help you to maintain the observer as an inner onlooker and to strengthen your capacity in this direction without being distracted.

Then open your eyes.

The observer or witness, awakened through the attention, holds the "room" that the content of thinking is filling. This is the result of the moon path, utilizing the past to enter the present. To turn toward the spiritual world, we have to open the doorways of the observer witness; the doors of the room must be opened to let in new, living spiritual thinking. It is meditation that opens the doorways or

portals in the room of the observer, the faculty of thinking, thereby allowing the in-streaming of spiritual thought.
This occurs though achieving empty consciousness in
meditation, where one's inner activity is awake but there is
no content.[1] This ability to surrender to opening the door
is now the sun path, the path to the light, warmth, and life
of the spiritual world, which are the esoteric symbols for
what we may participate in spiritually as wisdom, love,
and strength.

Having a clarified experience of the observer, of the
room in which we are thinking, before we open the doorways to the in-streaming of spiritual thoughts is necessary
if we wish to be fully conscious of our relationship to the
spiritual world. Once we become open to this in flow, the
thoughts that now think in us may at first seem far more
living than the thinking we are used to; they may seem
to be creative, insightful. These thoughts make connections that become an education for us. We begin to be able
to think with something wiser, as though wisdom were
thinking with us.

> Let us make clear to ourselves what is really brought
> about by meditation. Streams of spiritual life are always
> flowing through the world. These streams cannot flow
> into us when we are thinking about everyday things. But
> our meditation words are like portals that are to lead us
> into the spiritual world.[2]

There is another step that can be taken by the seeker
once the capacity to open the doors to the room has been
achieved and is under the seeker's control. This third step,

which is best taken only once the seeker or student is fully prepared, is, at will – or through the spiritualized-strengthened will – to dissolve the walls of the room entirely. This free will is a will to surrender, a will to self-annihilation as a personal particular self, and this is very difficult to achieve for the industrialized interiority, as it requires one to have purified the strengthened "self-rewarding will" that has been indoctrinated into the interiority. It requires an intensified devotion to something that is not our personal self and a capacity for devotion to that which we will not personally gain from.

The seeker who can achieve this may have now found the way to the new, conscious life in the spiritual world as it opens up beyond the "room." This third step – to open, to dissolve the walls – requires training and time, but once the meditant can achieve this out of the preparation of building the bridge, a new life begins – one that can no longer be forgotten. It changes how we see the earthly world, the meaning life has for us, and all that we now feel the impulse to work toward doing in the world. This is not a quick path; the bridge is built step by step, plank by plank, and much is learned about the nature of the self in its building.

This "self-knowledge" is one of the gifts of the path, even though through it we learn all sorts of things about ourselves that we would perhaps rather not know. This knowing has a great and necessary purpose.

The moon development is one half of our awakening; the sun development is the other half. Both developments only take place when we are present on the earth, the place where we as a humanity progress and evolve.

Self-development takes us from the personality to our humanity. Meditation takes us from our humanity to our spirituality. In order to understand the path to the spirit – the sun path – in its fullness, we cannot attempt to do so from the personality directly. Some personalities have the indoctrination or the education of being a "spiritual person." However, it may be that this self-image comes not from direct knowledge but rather from the intellectual content of spirituality; in that case, spiritual thoughts and conditions are filling our inner space automatically. To access a free spiritual life, we have to undergo developmental steps leading to our humanity in a way that overcomes all automatic tendencies.

On the path of moon schooling, we transform the past, the hereditary elements; on the path of sun schooling, we awaken the future, the universal. The bridge between these two paths is our humanity that works in the present moment. The observer or witness only becomes a persistent or continuous observer for the individual who has developed themselves through many years of practice. Until the observer is a consistent presence in our daily life, we generally resort to the automatic personality. This personality slowly transforms from being a content-filled personality with a conditioned or educated thought life, to one that is self-determined through the ongoing practice of self-development and self-education.

This path is walked in freedom and out of one's own resources. However, many individuals report experiences that seem to mimic or imitate the path of development and our resulting relationship to the spiritual world – that seem to mimic the results of either the sun training, the moon training, or both – through the use of consciousness-altering substances.

For instance, users of cannabis and those who study its experiential effects report the experience of gaining an observer-like capacity, the experience of being an onlooker to their own thought world or to themselves. This often gives rise to being able to let go of the everyday self and concerns. And many also report that simultaneous to this experience, or in place of it, they experience a more connected in-flowing of universal or "big-picture" thinking. The thinking opens up to concepts that are not of the personal, limited nature – concepts that grow and expand to illuminate the thinker beyond the usual materialistic boundaries. People can experience a kind of shared thinking-experience instead of the separated and subjective thinking content that is common to them in ordinary consciousness. They perceive the cannabis "doing the thinking," and this kind of thinking is beyond what they personally can think without it; it appears more creative, less confined to the known conventions, allowing them to think "outside the box." They experience having thoughts that "blow their mind," thoughts concerning realities that go beyond what we usually think about the world and life.

This dual development of having an observer perspective that is not bound, in its identity, with the content of thinking, and of perceiving the inflowing of more connected, unifying thinking, is for many people the experience of cannabis – and, further, they experience that it provides this dual development outside the path of one's own efforts.

It stimulates the observer and at the same time opens the door to the inflowing of the spiritual nature of thinking. Cannabis achieves this for the user, without the user having to do anything but ingest the plant in a form that retains its THC content, the active consciousness-altering element. It is useful to note that for long-term users, the amount of THC often needs to be increased in order to produce the same effects. Between the 1960s and today, the typical THC levels have greatly increased in the bred plants from 4% to as high as 34%. A new user will be introduced to much higher THC levels in the plant today as compared to the past. Although cannabis is classified as a hallucinogen, which means it will also affect the stimulation of the experiencing interior, it is still reported to have its strongest effects on the observer-consciousness and the thinking, whereas the effects of other psychedelics primarily influence the experiencing interior and the feeling life.

We can understand the prevalent use of cannabis in our time as an attempt to palliate the intellectual cage or the literal mind that the industrialized interior self is stifled with. We no longer live in the midst of a creative connection between our thinking and the thoughts streaming out from the things in the world. We are enclosed within the tower of the intellect, a condition for which we know we need to find healing. Getting high is a way of momentarily liberating the individual from this industrialized interiority. We have created a world that we need to remove ourselves from, but the industrialized interiority prevents us from doing this with ease, so the temptation to seek out something that can do this for us is all the greater.

Just as the observer is the capacity, the room, in which I think, so developing the experiencing interior now enables the feeling life to work as an instrument that can facilitate a more objective relationship to the world outside of me. In so doing, I am no longer in sympathy and antipathy with the world on account of conditioned responses or my personal biography. For instance, if we were to look at the rising sun and let it affect our inner experience, our inner world now moves differently through the activity that the rising sun reveals as compared to if we were to look at the rising moon. My experiencing interior world becomes an instrument of perception that allows me to view objectively what streams from the thing I perceive, in place of the usual scenario of my conditioned or personal reactions dominating my inner response. The personality will have a conditioned reaction, an automatic response, to most things, and the thinking in turn affects the feeling, which in turn affects our actions; thinking, feeling, and willing work and react upon each other within the automatic self. Along with the observer as the objective room in which the content of thinking works, the experiencing interior can become a receptive instrument that does not mix in its personal reaction with the experience that it is receiving. It allows us to have knowledge of the world in a rich and powerful way because the effects of the world express themselves *as they are* rather than as we want to see them.

Developing an awakened and clarified experiencing interior, the experiencing self, is also a part of the path. In our age of industrialized interiority, for most individuals this interiority has become a dulled, blunted instrument that works primarily on the basis of personal preferences rather than as an awakened sensitive instrument that experiences the power of what lives in the experience of the other. Today, personalities can look upon the vastness of the ocean and feel nothing. They can see the rising sun and be unstirred by it. Not only is the instrument of the experiencing interior blunted and dulled, but the guardian of the intellect blocks this capacity's ability to let in the world. The intellect has become the blunting instrument of our experiencing life. An essential part of inner development is to gain not only an objective capacity to experience the world around us, but also to sharpen this instrument so that it can have greater depth of experience and more refinement in the activity of understanding the hidden language that the world speaks. Those who have a hypersensitive experiencing interior invariably experience this sensitivity in a subjective or personal manner. An experiencing instrument that is self-developed allows for greater perception of the other, not a greater sensitivity toward gaining our personal desires and preferences.

Most people with an industrialized interiority are not hypersensitive, and for this reason inner development requires keeping at bay the blunting nature of the judging and labeling intellect. Therefore, having a capacity to observe is helpful in lessening the onslaught of the habits of this materialistic tendency and the deadening nature of literal thoughts.

Through inner development, our common emotional and feeling life is transformed into an experiencing instrument. Through meditation, the portals or doorways are opened so that we may now experience the spiritual realms not only through the connectedness of spiritual thinking but also through the activities of the spiritual life, giving rise to a new level of understanding and meaning for the events of the external world.

In meditation, the experiencing interior knows beyond the shadow of a doubt that the spiritual world and other consciousnesses exist because it experiences them for itself. As much as it can experience the activity behind things of the sense world, it can likewise experience the activity within the spiritual world that has no sense-perceptible manifestation. The observer is able to have spiritual thought, connected universal insight, and wisdom, but the experiencing interior is able to have a spiritual relationship and to perceive the relationship between various consciousnesses; this allows us to receive not only the insight, but also the understanding and meaning inherent within what is perceived. The experiencing interior, through meditation, feels all that presents itself to the inner world in color, form, and sound. In this way, we are able to be deeply moved by our inner experience, which can bring us to feel that what we experience through this realm is even more real than the sense world.

Many seekers upon the path may experience intensive inner visuals. At first these may give rise to confusion, as these visuals arrive from both the subconscious and picture-forming dimensions of the spiritual realm. Without the developed will, the seeker can do nothing but endure the bombardment. But through the developed will, the seeker is able to act in the inner realms and enter, through the visual manifestations, into the more clarified spiritual realms.

The psychedelics affect the human being differently. When somebody takes psychedelics of the serotonergic group, whether it be LSD, psilocybin mushrooms, DMT/ayahuasca, or mescaline/peyote, they thereby induce the sensitivity of the experiencing self. Lysergic acid diethylamide, better known as acid or LSD, is possibly the most well-known of the psychedelic drugs. Psilocybin causes an increase in empathy, euphoria, and altered thinking. In some species, it can cause open and closed-eye visuals. N,N-Dimethyltryptamine, better known as DMT, was introduced more widely by researchers in the late 20th century. Scientist Rick Strassman studied it extensively in the 1990s and gave it the nickname "the Spirit Molecule." DMT has been used for possibly thousands of years by Amazonian and other tribes; these tribes activate the DMT that is found growing naturally in a certain rainforest plant by brewing it in a tea called ayahuasca. This tea is then brewed together with other plants that contain what is known as MAOIs, which are an ingredient needed to enable the DMT to remain active when ingested by the human being. This substance may be among the most potent psychedelic drugs on earth, with the side effect

of powerful visual hallucinations. Mescaline is a psychedelic alkaloid that is found in a number of southwestern
cacti like peyote, the San Pedro cactus, and the Peruvian
torch. Peyote is an aspect of Native American shaman-
ism in some religious ceremonies. Mescaline causes color
enhancements, euphoria, and an increase in introspection.

People with an industrialized interior who ingest these
psychedelics often report having personal epiphanies
through the plant. There are other hallucinogens being
developed regularly in labs around the world that are not
arising from the plant world. It is said that new drugs are
entering the market every day. Although they are of different origins, there are a number of common experiences
produced by the hallucinogens. The user may no longer feel
dulled and blunted by the limitations of the personality's
common experience. Because the substance frees us from
the body-bound feeling and intellect, the experiencing
instrument is heightened by the chemicals and at the same
time the doorway to the picture-forming realm is opened.
In this way, an influx of experiences begins to flow in that
is an expression in spirit of the external appearances of
the manifested and un-manifested physical world. These
psychedelics give us the experiencing instrument and open
the door to a spiritual influx of a certain kind.

It is understandable that in our industrialized interiority, more individuals are medicating themselves or self-
medicating, even in the form of "micro-dosing," as a way
of managing the inner void that is so present for them, or
to manage the feeling-discord of anxiety, loss of creativity,

and general emotional malaise. Many users of ceremonial psychedelics also long for the community experience or the sense of belonging that they find through participating in deep inner experiences with others. Some people therefore find themselves having to take the substance even if they do not want to, just so that they can be a part of the gathering of seekers looking together beyond the sense world. The need for honest connection to self and others, to be united through experience, seems to play a big role in many of those who partake in these consciousness-altering substances. Communities are even being formed around taking substances, showing once again how the industrialized interior life has changed how we think, how we feel, and what we do together.

This inducing of the experiencing instrument and the opening of the doorway to spiritual experiences is quite different for those who have had their experience brought about by a plant than it is for those who have done so for themselves by ordering their personality and working consciously with meditation. The greatest deceptions arise through using substances in this way because when the personality has not been ordered, it infiltrates the spiritual in-streaming of experiences and alters the spiritual activity's ability to express universal laws and truths with clarity. Instead, those laws and truths are expressed in a clouded way, adulterated by the personal preferences and the conditioning of the individual. We therefore do not find ourselves in the united spiritual schooling of wisdom, love, and strength, but rather a personalized schooling primarily built on the nature of our own personal interior world that is full of conditioning. The subconscious is on the stage, inducing personal hallucinations. Genuine spiritual experiences do not produce personal revelations, because the spiritual world is not about you personally. Progressive spiritual experiences speak of the collective path of humanity; and through meeting these experiences by the efforts of our individualized forces of free will, they strengthen us with the capacity to engage in humanity's progression.

> The human being must become a partaker of the spirit in order to carry its revelations into the physical world. Human beings transform the earth by implanting in it what they have ascertained in the spiritual world. That is their task. It is only because the physical world is dependent upon the spiritual, and because human beings can work upon earth, in a true sense, only if they are participants in those worlds in which the creative forces lie concealed – only for these reasons should they have the desire to ascend to the higher worlds.[3]

The basic activity of stimulant-type substances – cocaine, methamphetamine, and amphetamines – is to induce a strength in the will impulses. They initially produce confidence and happiness, the tendency to be more talkative and feel more energetic, and increased sex drive and self-determination. This is often a type of drug that tempts either those who want to gain the power to push ahead within industrialized systems, or individuals who feel disenfranchised by the industrialized system and are attempting to reclaim some form of personal power.

With all use of consciousness-altering substances, our limited personal will is overridden by an enhanced will-activity of the drug. With the stimulants, this can give rise to opening the door to a will capacity beyond what is commonly accessible to the human being. Opening the door to the will, without training, can engage forces that have recourse to a capacity that enhances the human will. It is important to note that the synthesized nature of stimulant-type substances works even more destructively upon the individual's free will than substances that are not synthesized. Stimulant-based drugs are unlike other plant-induced experiences, which merely weaken the free will of the user; stimulants start to destroy this free will, and this makes them highly addictive. We see reactions such as self-destructive habits, picking, the scratching of one's skin without being able to stop, and other habits such as teeth grinding or compulsive activities, all to the point of self-destruction.

Opioids have an opposite effect to the stimulants, although their entry-point is also the body-will connection. They act by releasing the individual from the consciousness of being restricted and in pain in any part of their being, through loosening the body-will connection. The individual's will is quickly replaced by the will of the drug, promising comfort and ease. Again, this is highly addictive, as the habits are created by the chemistry of the substance through overriding existing habits and intentions within the individual's will. It is rarely utilized for spiritual experience, but it can be sought out for seeking the spirit, as it produces euphoria and so called "heaven"-like comfort.

Alcohol does not induce any of the faculties required to experience spiritual realities. Alcohol does nothing to open up those doorways, but rather it increases the thoughts, feelings, and will-impulses of the personality while at the same time increasing self-confidence, overcoming unsociability, and overcoming inhibitions. This has quite a different effect for the user; it enhances the personal automatic self and runs counter to developing perceptions that arise by moving beyond oneself; it closes the doors. At one time in the evolution of human consciousness, alcohol may have been a leading force for certain peoples moving out of the group-identity and into a self-oriented one. Today, alcohol has been found to be one of the top contributors to the reduction of happiness within relationships between people who consume it.[4]

When an individual develops the free will capacity out of themselves, they often feel supported, strengthened, and able to give more and achieve more in service to the world's progression. They experience a resource or a strength enabling them to take on and meet the world with a level of resilience and fortitude that isn't common to the personality and the automatic self. This resilience has been noted in various ways; those with a devoted spiritual life have more resilience in dealing with the struggles of life and a greater capacity to continue encountering challenges.

In the past, the need to develop all capacities was not essential, as is the case today. There was a consciousness of the spirit that resounded in the individual's hereditary element in ways that are impossible to find in the industrialized consciousness of our present age. And then there was always a guide, a guru, or a master to correct our strivings on the path and make up for what the candidate could not do for themselves; and the training was so rigorous that only advanced candidates could traverse it to the degree of the sun path.

The emphasis on the development of the observer is often a part of Eastern meditative practices. The development of the observer can be seen through the Eastern practice of mindfulness, Zen, and yoga, which utilized conscious activity in the body in order to give rise to the observer self. Through directing the thinking capacity into the body, the observer becomes awakened. Later, cults and other schools arose that focused on developing the experiencing soul through the path of devotion to the other. The devotee opens themselves entirely to the in-streaming that the teacher gives them. Through love and devotion to another human being, a "guru," or a divine spiritual being as in the path of religious devotion, the soul opens to the spiritual experiences. Then we see initiation schools of the will. Many of these schools work on the path of the will by means of ritual and inner re-enactments of spiritual reality that are brought about through extensive will-training – for example, intensified concentration. This has been the direction of many of the Western practices, and those participating take upon themselves the practice of the will to do the spiritual good in life.

Today, however, we are at a stage in our development where the individual seeker whose heredity is industrialized needs to cultivate an individual relationship to all three faculties. This is because in our time, we are only able to enter into the spiritual world and attain a conscious foothold if all three are present. An entry into realms that, in the past, were only accessible to the chosen few is now possible for the many. In the past, full development was only given to the initiates, the chosen few, and the religious path was given to the many; today a new possibility awaits humanity, as we are all able to cultivate these three new capacities.

The individual, through self-assessment, ensures that the observer-consciousness, the experiencing interior, and the free will are all developing and working harmoniously together. In the spiritual world, these three capacities will naturally separate. This can be a direct experience on the part of those who have already developed these human faculties consciously out of themselves. These faculties are experienced as being loosened from each other. The personality must continue to integrate their thinking, feeling, and willing together, albeit unconsciously. If this is not possible in the healthy personality, then imbalances arise. At the point where these three processes – the observer, the experiencing interior, and the individualized will – are cultivated to such a degree that we can experience them as three clarified faculties, the individual can then look upon their personality, this automatic self, as though they are looking upon an external being.

This benefits the seeker because they become fully aware of what is arising out of the personality and the automatic self. They know what is streaming from their own personality, and this allows them to gain clarity in differentiating this personal streaming from what streams from the spiritual world in its purity. Without the loosening of these three forces, the personal conditioning and education becomes mingled or meshed together with the inflowing of spiritual truth and spiritual realities, which means that under these conditions our supposed spiritual insights are merely personal insights leading to developing a spiritual personality. It means that our spiritual experiences become personal experiences, and the spiritual strength that is gained is now used for personal gratification. The stage of development of the moon stream allows us to differentiate between, on one hand, the personality and the automatic self, and on the other, the human faculty that can open doorways to the spiritual stream without muddying or distorting this stream with what is merely personal.

Some individuals embark on the path of self-development purely out of the impulse of self-motivation and self-progression, and in this case the human faculties they discover have been employed once again by the personality for self-oriented means. We can see this approach in books like "Mindfulness and Money," as well as a newfound focus on working the stock market as seen in articles on "Mindfulness and Trading." When an individual has a capacity for a strengthening or clarification of their observer-self, when they have a capacity for experiencing what is being spoken

behind the external appearance of things, and have a fruc-
tified power in the will, then this capacity can be employed
for even greater selfish attainment. That is why, esoterically, we never truly learn about the path of the moon
without also learning about the path of the sun.

> The idea that another person could be for us merely an
> object of observation must never, even for a moment,
> take hold in us. Hand in hand with every esoteric obser-
> vation of human nature, one must bring self-education:
> the fully mature inner ability to unreservedly value every
> individual, and to look upon what dwells in each human
> being as something holy, as something untouchable by
> us, even in our thoughts and feelings.[5]

If, on the other hand, only the path of the sun is taught,
then the individual is more likely to develop a mystical
relationship to the spiritual world. The mystics can indeed
gain cognition of spiritual life and spiritual realities, but
they are unable to bridge these realities in a way that makes
them useful for earthly progression. Again, in such cases
the mystical life serves the purpose of individual exploration rather than being of use for the many.

The stage of the loosening of the three faculties is
followed by a stage of further separation. In the spiritual world, the human being becomes three as the spirit
becomes one. If this separation occurs without the harmony of those three forces being cultivated, then it also
leads to the same distortions that can occur when we
"gatecrash" these realms through substance use.

Although the developing of all three faculties may not
appear to be necessary at the beginning of the path – since

one can gain a recognition of spiritual reality through any one of those faculties – nevertheless, as soon as we become active in the spiritual world we become aware of the necessity of building all three. The consequences of a partial development become clear through the struggles encountered by the student of inner development, but these consequences are amplified in the struggles of those accessing the spiritual world via substance use. Far fewer people go astray in the spiritual world through a one-sided development in their training than through the gate crashing or forced door-opening that the use of substances provides.

As a society, we are becoming more fully aware of the behaviors arising in users of stimulant-type substances (like crystal meth), such as violence, self-destructive tendencies, and rushing from one unbridled action to another (actions like scratching the skin or other actions that have no purpose, but that cannot be stopped). The power attained by substances like this ruins the user, and the corrosive effects in the realm of moral action has been noted by many. Psychedelics can lead us to an experiencing self that is filled with sentimental emotionalism, in which the feeling life dominates and independence is lost. It is well-documented that cannabis often leads to experiences of paranoia when the observer and the personality are made to exist together not through self-development, but through substance-development. The individual then becomes addicted to spiritual knowledge through the in-streaming of spiritually connected thinking, but without the capacity to will anything into the world.

It is essential for the student that the three fundamental soul forces – thinking, feeling, and willing – should have undergone harmonious development before being released from their inherent connection. . . . For once a mistake has been made and one of the soul forces falls prey to unbridled excess, the higher soul comes into existence as a miscarriage. . . . The unrestrained force pervades the individual's entire personality and for a long time there can be no question of the balance being restored.[6]

Religious and cultural substance use is often the reason people feel encouraged to take these so-called "plant medicines," and with the science of medicine using some of these plants for medical mind-altering purposes, they are also being given a "thumbs up" to the seeker of knowledge from this field. We must realize that the constitution of the indigenous peoples who used these substances is different from our own. They have not been tarnished by the impact of the industrialized world on their thinking, feeling, or will impulses. They can afford to utilize the plant wisdom because they are still spirit-wise in the original sense. This is very different from the spirit-devoid industrialized inner world that utilizes spiritual thoughts as a new commodity, with the accompanying sense of self-enclosure and separateness.

Extracting wisdom from the plant world can only be done today by the individuals or groups that have not become materialists or adulterated by materialism through their hereditary line. For most people, the time of passing on hereditary wisdom is over. The unconsciously gained moon-wisdom cannot help those individuals who are required, by virtue of their education, to seek an independent relationship to the spirit. The industrialized consciousness cannot return to its old state. The societies that inaugurated and perpetrated the hold of industrialized consciousness upon humanity must proceed forward and attempt to repair the past damage they have done to the planet and to other cultures. Regardless of the society into which we are born, we are all called to contribute to its progress with wisdom, love, and strength. We will once again unite the different peoples and streams into one humanity.

> We are a bridge
> between our past
> and future existence;
> the present a moment,
> the moment as bridge.
> Spirit grown soul
> in matter's enveloping sheath
> comes from the past;
> soul growing to spirit
> in germinal spheres
> is our future path.
> Take hold of the future
> through the past,
> hope for what's coming
> through what became.
> So grasp existence
> through growth; so grasp
> what's growing in what exists.

—Rudolf Steiner[7]

The evolution of consciousness is a concept that has been held throughout the inner spiritual traditions of many of the Western and Eastern approaches, although the language used to describe this is often different in the various schools of thought. The main idea is that the human being is evolving toward a fully conscious, awakened, and perfected 'I'-being.

In this way, the evolution of consciousness stands separately from the common understanding of humanity's evolution. This common understanding has been constructed and taught through the history of human endeavors and becomes a history of ideas, whether this be the history of economics or politics, or even philosophy, religion, or the arts. The education we receive with regard to this history is tainted by the biases of the society that presents it and by certain groups that wish to maintain power within those societies, and it informs the surface-level changes in humanity's outer reality. It also professes a kind of superiority of the new over the old ways of being and living. It is a history burdened with errors because it is not a picture of the whole; rather, it is a collection of pictures of parts that are being raised and revered as a totality by certain groups within certain races and cultures.

We have seen how this one-sided appraisal of humanity's development often diminishes certain races or cultures, or excludes them from active participation in shaping the "mainstream." This one-sided history can of course be justified by each group as a form of self-evaluation, if only they would be honest about the group they serve through the accounts given as history in a particular race or culture. Through this honesty, we would then be able more easily to recognize that the account is only a partial picture, and that another group, race, or people's account is just as important and valid.

Many individuals today are becoming aware of these hidden realities of certain races and cultures, and are bringing them forward, recognizing that the egocentric, Eurocentric reality that has dominated our general world-view has destroyed other worldviews in its persistent self-serving advancement.

> We must learn to live together as brothers or we will die together as fools.
>
> —Martin Luther King Jr.[8]

However, if we are to observe the term "evolution of consciousness," we are not seeking to describe a history of a particular group, but rather an account of the changes in the collective human consciousness that can be found by looking upon the changes within humanity as one unified people. In this way, our collective evolution can be observed in the universal development of the capacities of the individual human being across all races and cultures, irrespective of the race or culture itself.

> In our critical thinking as physicists or philosophers, we imagine ourselves set over against an objective world consisting of particles, in which we do not participate at all. In contrast, the phenomenal, or familiar, world is said to be riddled with our subjectivity. In our daily, uncritical thinking, on the other hand, we take for granted the solid, objective reality of the familiar world, assume an objective, lawful manifestation of its qualities such as color, sound, and solidity, and even write natural-scientific treatises about the history of its phenomena – all while

ignoring the human consciousness that (by our own criti-
cal account) determines these phenomena from the inside
in a continually changing way.[9]

The changes of our consciousness become the changes in
our world. These world changes – such as industrialization –
affect the environment, which affects the human body
and develops mutations in the DNA, which affects the
gene pool for the next generation. The body becomes
the ground of our work toward transforming the past, but
the spirit is the source of the future. This process of transitioning from being at one with the realities of the spirit
to being separated from spirit has taken place for many in
our world. Healing for the world arises by uniting with the
spirit again, through traversing the pathways necessary to
awaken the consciousness that can work with the health
of humanity.

It is a given that even these ideas of human development
may well be described very differently in these various cultures, and we must be fully aware that we can only describe
the evolution of consciousness in the context of our particular education. Even in the realm of language, we are
bound to a partial, educational view. Therefore, it is up to
those working from the various streams of thought to form
a bridge between the language presented in each schooling
path and their own experience, if they see a use or purpose
in doing so. As this book clearly focuses on the evolution
of consciousness as given in the esoteric schooling for the
industrialized interiority, it may be useful only to cultures
that have been lost to an industrialized interiority.

Without needing to dissect history, the way we look at ancient texts, and the ways of being of early humanity, we can still readily recognize that the original state of human consciousness from ancient times appears to be vastly different from the state of consciousness that most human beings experience today. In these ancient texts, we see various expressions of the human being that have no sense of separate existence within their group, no sense of individualized selfhood. A collective consciousness and group identity was the common expression of human consciousness for the majority of peoples walking the ancient earth.

However, today for most peoples the individual self-consciousness and our self-identity are regarded as a normal and, from their point of view, a healthy way of being. Today, only a few groups remain in the world that still live within this collective consciousness and group identity in a way that retains any remnants of that past state in which the whole of humanity once resided.

Still earlier, before the dawning of the group identity, it is said that the human being lived in a consciousness of unity, immersed as it were in the all-pervasive presence of the spirit. Owen Barfield, the British philosopher who traced the evolution of consciousness through the origins and development of language, describes the original state of human consciousness with the term "original participation," a unity and oneness with the cosmic consciousness that was recognized simultaneously as the divine consciousness.

Our experience of original participation was an experience of being at one with the spirit, and yet our awareness of this oneness was lacking and we were subjugated to a higher power. There was no ability to express the nature of self in full independence and freedom. For many, our present participation in the realm of consciousness is to be at one *only with ourselves*: awakened to our individualized existence, separated from the other, from the divine unity, and yet free to seek or not to seek the light of the spirit.

Most who are educated in this understanding will state that this is all part of the divine plan: for the human being to bring into existence the freedom to love or not to love. Love and freedom are, from this perspective, the very purpose of evolution, the meaning of existence itself, and therefore they must be guarded. This process – from being at one with the realities of the spirit, to being separated, to freely uniting again – is the necessary pathway.

Our destiny is to become both conscious and free.

—Owen Barfield[10]

The vast majority of human beings who walk the earth today experience consciousness not as a unity or even as a group identity, but as an individualized identity. This growing experience has led us toward a sense of isolation that has never existed in the collective human experience before now. In the modern world, it is this separation that causes us to seek beyond the state of separateness. In this way, the seeker of the light of the united spirit always begins the journey in the dark.

Initiation, as outlined in the idea of the evolution of consciousness, is not the same as the initiation rites that have taken place through outer, practical forms. When a child reaches puberty, they may be taken into traditions and into an initiation practice or rite of passage. These traditions focus mostly on the outer being of the individual and its relationship to community life. The initiation connected with the evolution of consciousness focuses on the individual's capacity to evolve in their consciousness beyond the present mass-consciousness experience, and in this sense to awaken the next step for the whole group or stream within which they are assigned to work.

The great initiates of ancient times are those who could bridge the revelations from the spiritual world to the physical world, and could thereby introduce great change and advancement into the group consciousness. These changes may affect the major leaps in human earthly development for that particular group, as well as beyond that group. In ancient times, these "royals" would be the leaders of the tribal group. These inner workings have later been described in our mythologies. The myths of the various ages help us to understand the interaction between the heavens and the earth, as well as the part played by various consciousnesses in that relationship of inner evolution leading to outer changes.

The emergence of the so-called great Western initiates came after a sequence of great leaps forward in humanity's consciousness brought about by Eastern initiates. These leaps brought humanity out of the "Self" in the sense of "God," to the "self" in the sense of "me, myself."

When the Western initiates arose, they had to hide the mystery schools from the effects of the necessary descending path that led away from collective God-consciousness. The initiation schools and meditative practices of the West are therefore little-known in comparison to the Eastern meditation practices and paths, which were developed in an age in which their practices were not under attack by a rising materialistic culture.

In the Western cultures, the initiates worked within the secret mystery centers. One of the last great outer mystery schools was the School of Chartres, where the cathedral still stands as the outer body for that inner training. In the various centers and the various streams of the mysteries, many different insights were taught and given, but there are certain aspects that they all have in common despite the variations in their individual thought, language, and expression.

One aspect common to all the groups was the knowledge of the cosmic or spiritual origin of all things. This became a new education beyond the knowledge of everyday life-experience. Another common theme that was taught throughout these centers is the reality of our past separation from this divine connection, and in turn a separation from the knowledge of our spiritual origin and of the spiritual origin of all things.

Today we are seeing an emergence of the need for the new mysteries. Today initiation is no longer a path walked by the chosen few, but it is now a path for the many; today we have the ability to develop the faculties to take ourselves forward. We are each being called, individually, to take a leap from where we are toward where we need to be in order that the collective consciousness can be accelerated at this challenging time in human evolution.

For the industrialized interiority, the age is over when the priest or guru stood between the spiritual world and the earthly life as "the only bridge" for others. The royals who ruled that age have, through the necessity of the spiritual evolution of humanity, given way to the cooperation of awakened individuals working together to create new agreements and forms. There is no longer a need for the few "royals," but now we need "the royal way," which necessitates individuals working together. In the initiation schooling, all who have the will to tread this way can now do so.

When a form from the past holds on beyond the period of its usefulness for humanity, it becomes an imbalance that works like a sickness. The fact that 1% of humanity holds the majority of economic power is a sickness we face. It is a distorted representation of the royals of the past age. Either blood or money puts them in this position, not the capacity for the royal way, which no longer needs pyramid leadership. The autocratic leadership method works against the royal way because only free human beings can walk this path of development. Even so-called innovative social media conglomerates are blocking others' freedom by utilizing autocratic methods within these new technologies, which could truly function in a positive way if they were made into instruments of collaboration and a true sharing economy. The past methods are trying to possess a new era; instead of working to heal our present sickness, they are making us sicker. The path for the peoples of the industrialized interior must now focus on self-development for world development.

One of the differences that might be expressed in certain inner development paths is that, from the point of view of the esoteric schooling, the world of the senses and our experience in the sense world – the so-called dual world of self and other – is purposeful. It is not just a "Maya" from which we should want to escape and detach ourselves; rather, the world around us actually has meaning. Even in our inner schooling and development, we can see how we are progressing by how we live together. There is also a third aspect: the relationship between self and other – two elements that can only appear because of the duality. The bridge between them is freely built, but all the potential to build it is given to us. When we are both free and conscious, then we can truly participate in the world's creating.

One of the greatest sources of meaning that the interior development path gives us to contemplate is that, as human beings at our present stage of development, we are working toward developing true freedom. Freedom is a paramount feature on the modern path of inner development. Hence, the idea of having a guru who could bring about a demanding influence on one's psyche goes against the path itself. Today new methods are needed that are self-directed, but not for self alone.

Freedom and the love of liberation comprise one of the great pillars of a genuine path for the industrialized interiority. But our habitual industrialized understanding of freedom is somewhat limited to the freedom to ensure that personal preferences are being fulfilled. The personality that is limited, and therefore unfree, cannot be the bearer of true freedom. Can a human being progress from the industrialized image of freedom to becoming a free being that can, of themselves, freely will, freely feel, and freely think, and through this freedom form a direct relationship to the spiritual world?

Most of us will be aware of this new, autonomous form of spiritual life from our own experience. The fact that it is so clarified in the renewed self-development schools is an indication of its importance within the inner development path. We are left to train ourselves to the point where we can begin our individual inner training through a direct connection with individual inner guidance. This, however, is not intended to lead to personal experiences of the spirit on account of this autonomous self, but rather it leads to an ability to remain self-aware in a united spiritual life while simultaneously bridging this spiritual wisdom, love, and life to the world in unique ways through each individual.

Seekers of the truth today are faced with many struggles. On one hand, for many people religious doctrines can feel dead and incapable of meeting the needs of our new interiority, especially if these doctrines are upheld without the element of religious renewal that leaves the individual free in their relationship with the spiritual world.

The seeker of today also has to steer themselves through the numerous paths on offer, as our global worldview of interfaith and inter-spiritual paths comes more and more into a unity. Those who seek beyond the realities of the sense world are not taking an easy path. They are not escaping the realities of this world, but they must endure all the snares and diversions that attempt to block a free relationship to the living spiritual world. In this age, it is easy to forget who we are and why we are here in this life. But we also need to know what we are doing and why we are doing it. The more insight we have, the more we are able to make our decisions by weighing, deep within ourselves, our individual relationship to what is being offered to us as a potential bridge to the spirit.

2

The Heart's Bridge

IN MANY PATHS, the work of the seeker is described as taking hold of our automatic personal selves and walking the path of self-transformation toward growing the divine self; this picture is also utilized in alchemy. The alchemist who seeks "the philosopher's stone" utilizes these interior development processes by means of external symbols. In alchemy, the moon path correlates to the substance of silver and the moon rules three domains within the body: the *brain*, the *skin*, and the *reproductive system*. These are the three stations of activity of our automatic selves. They are handed down to us through the hereditary line and inscribed into us through the collective community in which we are raised; in this way, they have now become tainted with industrialized tendencies for all people born into the industrialized interiority.

Our unfreedom lies in not having any mastery over these internal stations of our being. In our untransformed moon-selves, we think with *brain thinking*. This kind of thinking is a mirroring thinking; it is stimulated by reflecting what comes toward it. It is the kind of thinking a computer can perform, and, as we are coming to see, the computer is able to do so much faster than we can. Brain thinking reflects what has been given to it. We input the information, and this information can be recalled and even "rewired" together with other information by combining the thoughts that have been internalized; but this is not internally self-willed thinking. This "outer-world-educated" thinking is a thinking that is not free; it is automatic and it is stimulated by external effects.

Within the moon-feeling, we feel with *skin-feeling*. This hereditary skin-feeling means that we are sensitive to the things we are conditioned to be sensitive to. Only certain things touch us, and they do so because of our biography, our conditioning, our heredity. Our skin creates the boundary between ourselves and the outer world, and yet it allows us to touch and sense the world, experiencing what is outside us. But our skin also separates us from other individuals and categorizes us into races, thereby separating us into groups. Through the skin, the kin, we are conditioned to feel collectively about things. This, however, is a hereditary feeling that is handed down to us through blood, through culture, and through the feeling of "belonging" that these carry with them.

When we will from out of the forces of the *reproductive system*, we will to continue what is known – to reproduce again and again what is seen as normal to the outer culture of our particular world. We will from out of self-desire and we will for self-gratification, but this too has been handed down to us through the interiority of the collective. This will is inscribed in us through the hereditary line and our childhood education within a particular group-community; through this, we know what is expected of us in terms of what we could even want to will.

Each person is born with the foundation of three important inner faculties. From early childhood on, these faculties are awakened through the ground of a healthy development in terms of the way in which the senses interface with the external world (see *Spirit-Led Community*).[11] These faculties begin as the capacities for *attention*, *attachment*, and *self-regulation*, which are foundational for formal learning and independent learning. In adulthood, they become the pathway leading to the *observer consciousness*, the *experiencing interior life*, and the *free individualized will*. Each human being will have different capacities in one area or another. And not all capacities are equal in their function. Because of this, we may be drawn to one or another path of self-development, either because it speaks to what is familiar or to what is missing. However, ultimately we need to develop all three capacities, and they will need to be brought into a harmonious relationship with each other.

An individual who is entering into a relationship with the higher worlds without self-development, without moral development, can cause great disturbances in their own human organism. This is also the case if we pass the threshold leading into higher worlds without first balancing our three inner faculties. The disturbances can be so severe that they are hard to distinguish from what may be classified as psychological or mental illness. An unconscious meeting with the spiritual forces that both guard us and call us onward can leave many people with a heightened state of anxiety or depression. Anxiety and depression, in this sense, are a result of unconsciously encountering internal processes that we need to, but have not yet, transformed. In esoteric terms, this is known as the encounter with the guardian of the threshold. Today, we see many people suffering from anxiety and depression who haven't even been using substances, and this is one of the signs that humanity itself is moving unconsciously toward the world of the spirit without the necessary preparation.

The diligent student of the path likewise encounters these spiritual forces, but because the *observer-self* can distinguish them as being separate from the *experiencing self's* response to the encounter, this encounter therefore does not have the impact of disturbing the experiencing interior world in an ongoing way within daily life, or of bringing discord and disharmony into the inner world in other ways. It is well known that anxiety and depression are the side effects of many consciousness-altering substances. And those who have experienced such states tend to look for something that can take those feelings away. This can then lead to a need for more of the substance that originally caused the discord, in order not to feel anxious and depressed again, or to the use of a variety of other substances in order to manage the internal discord. Others come to recognize that it is time to stop using the substance, and that the substance "takes more than it gives."

However difficult this may sound, an unconscious encounter with the spiritual path, resulting in anxiety and depression, is also a very positive sign from the perception of esoteric development. This is because it indicates that your guardian has pushed you back from proceeding into realms that can create far greater imbalances, leading to conditions such as psychosis, mania, and/or drug-induced schizophrenia, in which case the individual would be classified with a clinical psychiatric disorder.

Cannabis is most likely to produce this side-effect of anxiety and depression because it is working with the induction of the observer self, but without any individualized will. Depending on the criteria that is being used for the assessment of addiction, cannabis could be seen as both addictive and non-addictive. Many would rather describe marijuana use, as with most other drugs, in the context of a spectrum; first, it can lead to the development of problematic use, known as marijuana-use disorder, and only thereafter is it classified as an addiction. Marijuana-use disorder identifies how the substance prevents the individual from carrying out the intentions of their own will. It is described how marijuana use leads to changes in choices and direction because the use of the plant overrides the intentions and life-commitments that the individual has made. Basically, the individual cannot stop using the substance even though it interferes with many aspects of their own life in ways that are in contrast to their own intentions. Cannabis is a less addictive substance than those that work directly into the will, where our habits are formed, and that affect the body chemistry; these are the stimulant-type substances like methamphetamine/amphetamine. However, the marijuana-use disorder is a more pervasive problem.

The hallucinogens, which have a greater effect on the experiencing interior, do not produce chemical addiction but rather an addiction to process and experience. The intensity of the "trip" is so vibrant, so real, that sometimes it can be described as more real than earthly life; daily life becomes grey in comparison to the psychedelic-induced world. And a desire to be living in that level of exalted intensity and experience, which cannot be found in the world of the senses, draws the individual back to the substance, creating an addiction to experience or an attachment to the process. On the other hand, many report being more emotionally sensitive in daily life, as though they are raw or vulnerable and less solid in the feeling realm, especially if they experience hallucinogenic flashbacks.

It is also apparent that without building the conscious bridge, many individuals find it incredibly difficult to integrate the experiences induced by the doorway of hallucinogenic substances. In the psychedelic trip, there is often not even full recall, and although of course people can take the substance to different levels, it is usually the push toward and through the hallucinogenic part of the trip that drives a person to use a higher dose, in order to induce a more intensive experience.

Integrating into everyday life what is experienced in these realms, understanding the laws of the spiritual world that must only be active in the spiritual world, and understanding the laws of the physical world that must be contained within the physical world, are a part of our education on the esoteric path of training. Even though the esoteric student may experience a feeling of oneness with the world through the meditation path, you are not likely to hear them express their experience in the sense world with words like "I am the ocean." This blending of the various realms of reality is a common sign of an induced or forced entry into higher realms.

In contrast, the esotericist is able to integrate their experiences in other worlds and at the same time not confuse or mix together the worlds in which they are participating. It is true that the esoteric student will likewise say that being spiritually awake in other realms is "more real" than experience in this sense-perceptible world. But there is no confusion in terms of which laws belong to which realm, nor is there an addiction to the other state of consciousness.

> One must always take into consideration that when the right path is pursued, behind every such experience another immediately arises. If the first experience is there, then the other cannot fail to appear. What one has to bear will immediately be accompanied by the power to really bear it if only one contemplates calmly and takes the time to notice what is seeking to reveal itself in one's soul. If something painful happens, and at the same time a feeling of certainty lives in the soul that there exist forces that can make the pain bearable and with which one can unite oneself, then one will reach the point of relating to such experiences – which would be unbearable if they were to occur in the course of ordinary life –

as if one were the observer of oneself in all that one experiences. For this reason, those who are on the path of suprasensory knowledge do inwardly live through the ebb and flow of many waves of feeling and yet show perfect equanimity in their sensory lives.[12]

It is a part of the schooling and training of the esoteric student to recognize the importance of self-development before entering these other realms. On the other hand, self-development without a relationship to higher knowledge can cause extended and inflated egotism. Inflated egotism is a hindrance that all seekers need to be aware of as a major challenge for the industrialized interiority. If we can imagine a human being who has developed the capacity of the observer self, who has refined the instrument of the experiencing-feeling interior, and who has gained strength in their free individualized will, but has no relationship to anything existing beyond the sense world, then there is a tendency for all this self-development to be used for the personal self. This temptation stands before the seeker as well. The path is the path. How we walk it and meet the necessary challenges upon it is all determined on the basis of our preparation. Moral development must exceed our spiritual development.

An atheist who engages in self-development could harness all of these self-development capacities and employ them for personal gain. We know this because it is clear that an individual can do mindfulness exercises without having any relationship to higher worlds or spiritual realities, and then employ the benefits toward self-accumulation in the sense world. On the esoteric path, knowledge of the higher worlds and inner development are given simultaneously, and in this way when the observer-self is developed, it is not bound only to the personal self, but awakens as a *faithful observer.*

This is not in any way connected to the blind faith of indoctrination by an outer authority. The awakened capacity of the observer is in no way blind, but it embodies a faithfulness in the unseen or a faithfulness that behind the sense-perception is a spiritual reality – a faithfulness in the fact that the spiritual world does indeed exist, a faithfulness that within the other being is a spiritual being that likewise develops into an observer capable of opening the door to the spirit. The self-control that serves to develop the observer is the same for those who recognize the higher worlds and for those who do not recognize them. The self-reliance that is developed through refining our own instrument of experience is also the same for those who recognize the higher worlds and for those who do not. For both, the individualized free will, through self-control and self-reliance, increases in its capacity. But for those who do not recognize the higher worlds, these heightened human faculties can increase egotism and thereby separate the individual even more from the united striving of humanity, through this enhanced egocentrism. Remaining isolated in self-oriented capacities on the path of selfhood is a danger for all developing capacities.

We can try this short exercise. First of all, repeat the "Is this I?" exercise (given in chapter 1 and abbreviated here) in order to establish the position of the observer within.

Is this I?

Experience the pressure of the chair against your body. Ask yourself inwardly, "Is this I?" This question is not meant to be answered, but it is an assistance to help us bring our attention to the things outside us, and by bringing our attention to them in this way, one reaches greater clarity as to the difference between the observer self and the self that I can look upon. By moving toward the observer and experiencing it, we are trying to induce the observer-force more strongly. Take a moment with each of these experiences before moving on to the next.

Observe the rising and falling of the breath. Ask yourself inwardly, "Is this I?"

Become aware of any sensations in the body. Ask yourself inwardly, "Is this I?"

Become aware of the sounds in the space around you and outside. Ask yourself inwardly, "Is this I?"

Become aware of the warmth of the body. Ask yourself inwardly, "Is this I?"

Bring your attention to anything that distracts you and ask, "Is this I?

Then open your eyes.

Once the observer is activated, look at the plant world and see if you can have an experience of purely looking on in the scientific manner of observation. Then add to that an experience of having faith that something other than what I can perceive with my senses is there within the plant, while at the same time continuing to look on with the capacity of scientific observation.

Those who have a natural relationship to the spiritual world may find it difficult to understand that many individuals can develop an observer that is completely separated from spiritual realties; this is because those who have this natural relationship tend to look toward the other with a natural faithfulness. But it will help us to understand the capacity itself, and the experiences that many individuals are having, if we can clarify the difference between the "observer" and the "faithful observer."

With the faithful observer, the doors to the spirit may not yet be opened. There may not yet be a direct perception of the in-flowing spiritual world of thinking, but there is a faith that it is there and will be there, and it will continue to grow as one progresses on the esoteric path.

The experiencing self can be developed by those who have a relationship to the spiritual world, but it can also be developed by those who do not have this relationship. On one hand, the experiencing-feeling interior, as described, develops into a sharpened instrument that can feel and experience what is streaming from the world in a deeper way.

And there are those who develop a sensitivity to the external world of experiencing by taking on an artistic training. There are also those who develop a sensitivity to the experiencing realm as therapists, counselors, and in other fields, where the need for an empathetic experience of the client's inner life requires an inner sharpening in order to do the task well. And there are those who develop a strengthened relationship to the experiencing interior by recognizing that the experiencing self works in two directions. These individuals know that not only can I allow the outer world to affect me more intensively – so that I experience a deeper sense of fulfillment from the beauty of nature as a result of my ability to connect with experiences of the world outside – but I also realize that I can change how I am feeling within, out of my own volition. For instance, some individuals work with positive affirmations in order to adjust not only their thoughts but also their own feelings. This has a strong power in terms of the individual's capacity of self-reliance; it has the power to change how we think and feel, and particularly how we feel inwardly. In this way, certain visualization exercises are utilized to adjust one's own inner feeling and experience, simply according to personal preference.

The individuals who take up those practices do so purely for themselves – as long as they do not feel the need to have a relationship to objective higher worlds. They can visualize whatever they wish to visualize, whatever makes them happy. We can participate in the various exercises of the New Age movement, and yet we can refrain from having a relationship to the realities of the spiritual world, developing instead a relationship to inner realities that we wish to experience for our own benefit. It can go so far that one thinks that angels do not exist for their own sake, but for my gratification; angels do not exist with meaning and purpose for themselves, but they exist to look after me and gratify me. The experiencing interior tunes in to the recognition that my thoughts and feelings engage other consciousnesses in order to get them to work on my behalf

– for example, making angels do what I want them to do. We see this in books like *The Secret*, where we attempt to utilize spiritual laws for self-gain.

Conversely, the experiencing-feeling life developed by the esotericist is intended to work as an instrument for objective perception and not for my own sympathy and antipathy, for my own preferences. It is not a training aiming to turn this experience into something I prefer, but rather it is developed as an instrument that can perceive the effects of things in the realm of harmony and disharmony. When the student has developed an ability to not judge or give preference to certain experiences, but instead to allow the experiencing instrument to inform them of the harmonious or disharmonious activity in what they are perceiving, then this in turn helps them to develop a capacity of bringing to the world that which creates harmony, peace, or love. And it helps them to do so not out of a personal desire to adjust this or that for one's own satisfaction and relief, but because participating in this activity supports the revelation of spiritual forces working out of wisdom and harmony in the activity of the world.

The individualized will can be developed through activities such as martial arts; it can be developed by any form of training where you engage your capacity to strengthen your free will. The strength of the individualized will gives the individual a position of power in the world because the individualized will can change outer circumstances and improve these circumstances for itself. This will can become our drive and ambition toward personal wealth.

This will can become our drive toward self-preservation, a drive toward orienting our life around our own personal health and wellbeing. And this will can be an effort toward just sustaining myself, for as long as possible, in the conditions I want to maintain.

These may be common goals for the industrialized peoples. But for those with the common capacity of will, which is increasing: as long as self-gain continues to be the goal, we will not have understood the will to the spirit, the will to the light. This picture reveals some of the most essential sources of meaning in life itself. Owen Barfield described humanity's evolution as progressing from being conscious of the spiritual world but unfree to reaching the point where we are now unconscious of the spiritual world but have free will. In this free will, we are free to choose to develop a relationship to the divine spiritual world, free to work on our own self-development and the acquiring of virtues; we can work toward developing the eternal being within. With free will, we are likewise free to use this power solely for a life dedicated to our own wealth, health, and sustained life.

So along with the faithful observer and the experiencing harmonizing interior, the esotericist works toward the free good will. On one hand, moral development of the personal self is essential to being able to recognize the good will that must be developed by choice in our age.

Instead of the will engaging itself primarily in pursuit of wealth on a day-to-day basis, the will to the light orients us toward seeking the divine. Instead of a fanaticism regarding our own health and a willingness to focus our efforts primarily in that direction, the will to the light seeks to develop virtues. And instead of putting all our efforts into sustaining and prolonging our own existence as we want it to be, through the path of inner development the will transforms the personal, transient self into the eternal, spiritual self.

Those on the path of self-development without a relationship to higher worlds could be led to spend all of their time, energy, and attention – all of the will forces they are developing – on seeking wealth, health, and prolonged life, thereby exacerbating the common condition of the industrialized interiority. This way of thinking about these three life-goals themselves needs to be unraveled, as the industrialized interiority has changed our perception of them. "Wealth" is no longer a communal gain for the flow of fortune between people, but has become a means of gaining power over others. "Health" has become the removal of symptoms that we do not want instead of a way of being in relationship to ourselves and others. "Prolonging life," with the goal of living life our own way until the very end, has taken precedence over a path of gradually surrendering our egotism with the decline of the physical body and focusing on building inner connections with the essential goal of having a fulfilling spiritual life.

With the awareness of the spiritual world, we use our daily life – our time, energy, and attention – toward developing a relationship with the divine, toward developing virtues, and toward self-transformation, so that the transient or personal nature is transformed into capacities of the eternal self. Although we see these three will-processes in the education given by various religions, on the inner path of our time these processes are not dictated by any outer authority; today, this development needs to be achieved in freedom. At the same time, this in no way means that one cannot find this freedom in the religious path one has chosen.

Because He Gave Birth
—Francis of Assisi

So
Precious
is a person's faith in God,
so precious;

never should we harm
that.

Because
He gave birth
to all
religions.[13]

In this time of the free individualized will, there is no one path to the divine that is bestowed by the blood-bond. In various traditions, the divine ideal is named accordingly; for Buddhists it would be Buddha, for Christians it would be Christ, for Muslims it would be Muhammad, for Pagans it may be Nature, and for others it may be Love. The important thing is that the divine ideal is something you have come to out of yourself. Your understanding of the divine works within you, orienting you toward a benevolent presence of spiritual life that expands beyond the personal self.

This divine ideal cannot be indoctrinated into us if it is to heal the unhealthy development of today's industrialized interiority. Each individual determines their divine ideal for themselves, through their own self-education, and utilizes this divine ideal in their daily orientation. This can take a long time for some individuals; and yet, for others, coming to know what the divine orientation is for them in their lives may be instantaneous. It can be very hard for those who have been indoctrinated into religions to freely find their divine ideal. But this divine ideal may also end up being the very same one that your childhood provided. It is important to contemplate your divine ideal because this will help you to orient toward the stream of spiritual support; and at the same time, it will help you to develop the thoughts and words that we need in order to convey to others our understanding as well as, if necessary, our spiritual experiences. The divine ideal is recognized in our experiencing interior because our contemplation of it brings an inner reverence and an upliftment from the personal to the spiritual.

In the age of the individualized will, the virtues that we recognize we need to develop are not to be insisted upon by some force outside of ourselves, but rather evaluated and determined individually. We have many expressions of the virtues to draw upon. Virtues correspond to the qualities that we would understand to be the living nature of our divine ideal. What is the Spirit or God for you? The question is asked not in regards to the religious indoctrination of wrath and rules, but rather in the sense of the divine ideal that you yourself turn to with reverence. For a Buddhist, the various virtues already conveyed through its path to nirvana may be the virtues that resonate with you, such as compassion, loving kindness, equanimity, generosity, acceptance, right conduct, etc. For those who recognize Christ as their divine ideal, the virtues such as sacrifice for the progression of the other, to love one another and to develop a capacity to love your community, charity, forgiveness, humility, temperance, and courage may speak to you. For Muslims, the virtues of hospitality, respect, tolerance, honesty, justice, modesty, fulfillment of promise, and patience may already align with your own understanding. In fact, all these various virtues can be worked upon by anyone. They all point to our common path of virtue development and they are indications of what we may need to develop individually.

The esoteric student must, for themselves, out of their own lives, determine the virtues that need to be schooled in them, rather than taking on an indoctrination that deems their actions to be right or wrong according to an outer authority. We can do this by assessing the difficulties that come to light in our interaction with the events of our individual lives – for example, a situation that we know we haven't met well according to our own ideals.

Exercise for understanding individual virtue development:

Think of a past event that still causes discord in you. Build a picture of what took place as vividly as possible, so that you can call up the internal discord again.

Then ask the question, "What virtue was that developing in me?"

Or: "What virtue, if I had it, would have allowed me to meet this circumstance differently?" "How would I meet this circumstance according to my own ideal?"

There may be other questions about the virtues that need to be asked, so that one can look at this circumstance from another angle. This may need to be done several times before clarity arises.

In this exercise, we can perceive a shift of focus in our inner training from one oriented around a collective stream comprising a group of people who need to develop certain virtues (such as has been dictated in the past), to one oriented around the depths of an individual biography that reveals exactly what is needed for one's own evolution.

Our divine ideal may not exist in an exalted spiritual being of the great religions. It may be something that we have awakened to through our lives. It is of the utmost importance that it is individually determined, because through this individually determined divine ideal, we begin to understand that developing virtues is a matter of developing ourselves toward the capacities of the spirit that we ourselves understand and seek. The understanding of virtues brings the events of our lives into a totally different context. If I saw the schooling of my biography as an evolution toward greater self-perfection, toward closeness with the divine world through my opportunity to develop virtues, then my biography may be understood differently.

The next step – the ability of each individual to transform the transient self into the eternal self – then begins its development. The understanding of this transformation is to be found in the esoteric knowledge that after the death of the personal self and all that belongs to it, only processes belonging to the spiritual world live on. The virtues that we develop, since they are a matter of spiritual activity, become a part of our eternal being. The will to align my own life – what I do outwardly and what I do inwardly – with the virtues of the divine that I myself have come to understand, becomes a self-directed schooling in spiritual development. Although many companions on the path may be undergoing this same schooling, it is not because it is handed to us by some external authority or even by a personalized unconscious authority, but because through our own knowing, through our self-education, and through our direct relationship with the spiritual world, we know for ourselves that it is a right and true schooling.

Every individual is required to undertake this process for themselves: determining their own divine ideal, contemplating the virtues that emanate as activity from this divine source, and then freely aligning their daily lives with this divine ideal. This can be done both by utilizing the "book" of our own life in order to recognize what needs to be transformed within us, and by practicing living and growing the virtues toward an individualized, free relationship to the spirit. These individuals can help themselves and others to correct their one-sided capacities by striving toward the three good-will activities. This can be a support to those who are affected adversely by one-sided development – both those who are at the beginning of the path of self-development and those who have done extensive self-development but are not employing it in relationship to the divine world.

There are also other exercises that support building this bridge between the automatic personal self and the divine realms. In a certain sense, this bridge is recognized in all traditions as the virtue or state of being belonging to the divine itself – and that is love. God is love, spirit is love; this is the common understanding of all the religions.

The three moon-organs are the brain, the skin, and the reproductive system. These three organs of our everyday orientation – in terms of how we think, feel, and will through these organs – are generally unconscious. By walking the path of inner development, we find the spiritual centers in the body within these organs. We move from the periphery of the organ to its internal center, and this greatly helps our ability to awaken the higher faculties of the observer, the experiencing interior, and the free will. In the past, before our industrialized interiority had developed, the three spirit-centers of the body represented the most useful pathway because it allowed us to come back to the pure capacity in its original, "God-given" form once we had cleared it of all conditioning and materialistic orientation. The "God-given" body comes from the past development of humanity and has been adapted and adjusted through the ages, generation after generation.

In the brain, the spiritual center is the pineal gland. This is the focus of many meditative practices of the past; it allows us to perceive the spirit activity within the body. The center of the experiencing interior is within the "internal skin" of the lungs. "Pneuma," meaning spirit, refers to the lungs as the internal skin that still touches the other through the shared air; in the past, breathing exercises were also a doorway to the spirit from within the body. The "Hara," or the area located just below the navel, is the bodily center for the will, and it is also the focus of most martial arts techniques and many meditative exercises that focus on the body/will connection. Developing strength in the moon transformation has been the primary focus for Eastern meditation techniques of the past ages; although there are many and various techniques, they all primarily end up focusing on one or more of these moon spirit-centers.

Today, we are in a different place because for the industrialized people these three centers have been affected by what is being recognized as engineered evolution. We cannot imagine that the changes to our consciousness brought about by the world have not also brought about changes to our bodies. The industrialized hereditary body that we now receive is not only "God-willed" but human-willed, and it will be ever more so as the industrialized world progresses through each generation. The three spirit-centers are different for the industrialized peoples, as awakening them does not keep us from utilizing them for selfish means. We therefore need to include, in the path of our awakening, the organ in us that is most resistant to the industrialized world – and that is the heart.

There is only one organ for the sun path, alchemically speaking, and that is the heart. The heart will eventually become the place where we are able to unite our thinking, feeling, and willing in direct relationship to the living spiritual world manifest in each heart. In the past, the pure spirit-centers of the moon path allowed us to think, feel, and will through the "God-given" bodily centers, which were bestowed upon us. This allowed us, indirectly, through the embedded bodily wisdom, to reach outside the common knowledge in order to gain spiritual knowledge. However, now we are able to find the bridge to the present living moment of our spiritual life within our present connection to our daily lives; each heart is a direct bridge to a living relationship with the spirit of the world.

In the heart
Lives a human organ
That of all the organs
Contains the most
Spiritual matter;
That of all the organs
Lives spiritually
In such a way
That the spirit manifests itself
The most materially.

Therefore the heart
Is the Sun

In the human universe;
Therefore it is in the heart
That the human being
In its being
Is most
In its deepest source.[14]

—Rudolf Steiner

The human heart is the center in which the living spiritual world and physical self unite within the human body. The heart is the great harmonizer, the great peacemaker. In the physical body, we see this human heart as a mediator and harmonizer between the sensory nervous system that takes in the surrounding world through the senses and provides us with our sensitivity organization, and the metabolic digestive system that transforms what is taken in and provides us with energy.

The heart may well be attacked by the agitation of the nervous system, whose rhythm is fast and wired, or through the metabolic digestive system that is overtaxed by overeating, poor nutrition, poor sleep, etc. But between these two, the heart holds a steady pace.

The heart does not wage war with the other systems; it does not induce imbalance, but seeks harmony, peace, and collaboration in its function within the other human systems. And it also seeks this harmony and peace, with its "un-warring" nature, in the inner life of the human soul.

The heart is the internal bridge in the human body. It is the bridge in our relationships, the bridge from one human being to another. And it is also our eternal bridge between the spirit and the world. Our individual human heart is the mystery center through which we participate in the collective progress of humanity. Strengthening the heart's activity on all levels supports the bridge in body, soul, and spirit. In turn, it supports the healing of the un-bridged experiences that have been induced by substance use. The strengthening of the heart restores balance and harmony and supports the circulation of the heart's life-giving gifts.

> In the temple of the human body is the holy of holies. Most people live in this temple without knowing anything about it. . . . Therein is the holy vessel. . . . One enters the mystery center of one's heart and a divine being arises from this place and unites itself with the divine outside, with the being of the spirit of the world. It is the mission of every single human being and of the whole of humanity to fill themselves with this spirit and to recognize themselves as a center living in this spirit through which the spiritual light and spiritual warmth can flow into the earth with strength, redeeming it and raising it into spiritual realms.[15]

Here are four exercises that can serve to support the heart-bridge on the various levels of being:

Exercise 1: To Support Bodily Rhythm and Harmony

The human rhythms of four heartbeats per breath and 18 breaths per minute mean that the heart beats 72 beats per minute. (This is reflected in the processional movements of the vernal sun, which moves one degree every 72 years.) Then, this amounts to 1080 breaths per hour, which results in 25,920 breaths per day. This number of breaths equals the number of years in a Platonic or Great Year, as was known by ancient wisdom; in modern astronomy, this is called the precession of the Equinoxes. Equinoxes happen twice per year: on March 21 and September 21, when day and night are equal in length. In between the Equinoxes we have the two Solstices at June 21 (representing the longest day and shortest night in the northern hemisphere, and the shortest day and longest night in the southern hemisphere) and December 21 (representing the shortest day and longest night in the northern hemisphere, and the longest day and shortest night in the southern hemisphere). Due to the precessional movement, the sun appears to move slowly around the stars of the Zodiac and completes its full circle in 25,920 years, which is a Cosmic or Platonic Year.

Take the rhythm of your resting pulse, which is quite a slow rhythm compared to the rhythm of our daily lives in the modern world. Once you have the beat of your resting pulse, practice walking for 15 minutes per day in nature to that beat. Even though the beat itself may increase while you're walking, try to maintain a pace of walking at the resting-pulse rhythm. We do this without a destination in mind, but purely allowing the rhythms of our own body to come into a unity with the rhythm of our heart. Don't carry anything in your hands, letting the hands stay naturally by your side. However, do this in a way that the fingers do not drop down unconsciously; rather, engage the fingers slightly as though you might be holding a stick, particularly in the right hand. The left hand in-streams the forces of the surrounding nature, while in the right hand a circuit is created with the thumb and fingers so that what streams in can enliven the depletion in the body and support the rhythms of the body through the rhythms of nature.

Exercise 2: To Support the Life-Giving Forces of the Heart

The plant world has a continuous connection to the cosmic spiritual forces. The plants themselves bridge the cosmic sun to the earthly core. They are mediators of the sun forces streaming into the earthly world. The trees are able to hold these sun forces within themselves, whereas other plants are purely bridging the cosmic and earthly connection. A particular type of tree, the evergreens, can maintain this life-bridge all year round, whereas deciduous trees build up those forces in the springtime and during the cycle of the full moon. Through our relationship to, and our work with, this kingdom, this bridge of nature, we can support the bridge of our own heart within our body.

The sun is the cosmic heart and the trees store the sun forces within them. We can access these stored sun forces and in this way enliven our own life forces, which support the heart's life-flow.

Take your left hand and place it behind the region of your heart (on your back), putting the palm on a tree that is healthy and in its own natural environment – ideally supported by a diverse ecological system. City trees would not be useful to work with for this exercise. With your feet placed hip-width apart, place your right hand above the solar plexus, between the heart and the solar plexus.

Having the body in the position of a pentagram activates the streaming of the ethers in the body. We breathe into our belly, up into our chest. Through this exercise, the heart can be filled by the sun forces that are held within the tree.

Exercise 3: For the Inner Development of Heart Forces

Utilizing this meditation verse is a powerful way of activating the heart center.

> I feel sunlight in my heart
> Sunlight turns to warmth in my heart
> My heart's force streams into my hands
> My heart's force streams into my feet
> My heart's force is a gift from God
> I will work with God's gift
> Thus may I hope to become strong.[16]

—Rudolf Steiner

In this exercise, as in all meditative work, we want to simultaneously *think and see* what we are doing with the verse, and, at the same time, to *experience and will* this to be the center of our inner activity. No other thoughts or distractions may enter into our inner world as we engage with esoteric verses. The first line, "I feel sunlight in my heart," is not an automatic tendency. Our tendency would be to see sunlight; but here, in the verse, we are asked to feel sunlight. So the heart is here used as an organ of experiencing activity. The second line, "Sunlight turns to warmth in my heart," is changing this feeling of light into a new activity. Esoterically, light is the symbol for wisdom. Warmth, esoterically, is the symbol for love. So in the second line, "Sunlight turns to warmth in my heart," there is a transformation. Now in the third line, "My heart's force streams into my hands," one keeps a conscious, active connection to the center of the heart while experiencing the activity that was developed through the first two lines radiates out down both arms and into the hands as a continuous stream. With the next line, "My heart's force streams into my feet," we take the activity built in the heart, and this activity streams down simultaneously into both feet, while it continues its streaming into the hands. In the next line, "My heart's force is a gift from God," we inwardly stream upwards toward the third eye. So we now have an internal pentagram of heart-forces streaming while at the same time holding our attention on the center of the heart. The soul-spiritual heart's center is not slightly to the left, as is the case with the physical heart, but it finds its center just above the solar plexus, above the tender, soft point where the two ribs meet, in the center of the chest. In the next line, "I will work with God's gift," we again come back to the heart-center, our heart, now in gratitude. "Thus may I hope to become strong."

Exercise 4: For the Spirit Activity of the Heart

Visualize a six-pointed star, which is one of the esoteric signs for the heart as well as one of the esoteric keys for entry into the higher realm of the spiritual world. The two interlocking triangles, "as above, so below," also represent the bridge. Here we have the triad of the human capacity to think, feel, and will, united with the triad of the spirit of wisdom, love, and strength. This symbol can be utilized for deep contemplation.

Then, from this symbol, visually make the lines of the six-pointed star continue onward, so that they stream out into infinity where they connect with all the other streams coming from the heart of each individual who also bears this sign. In this way, our hearts become linked with the hearts of all those on the path.

At the end of this exercise, enter into gratitude.

Gratitude is an important bridge between ourselves and the spiritual world. After every meditation, or every connection with the realities of spiritual life through the exercises, it is most useful to have a few minutes of gratitude for what we have just participated in. This gratitude has several consequences. To the spiritual world, it signifies the soul's recognition of its presence. But it also supports our inner world by working as an antidote to the personal striving for repeated experiences. Our industrialized tendency is to want to repeat a beneficial experience. We need to be active against the part of ourselves that wants, the next time we meditate or have a connection with the spiritual world, to experience exactly what we experienced before. This desire is the materialist in us.

Exercise 5: Uniting with Our Divine Ideal.
A Meditation Verse:

Evening:

Picture the heart and a small light in the heart; then inwardly speak these words:

Divine   light illumine me
Divine   power strengthen me
Divine   love warm me

Then enter into inner tranquility.

Morning:

Picture the sun outside shining upon me; then inwardly
speak these words:

Divine   love warm me
Divine   power strengthen me
Divine   light illumine me

Followed by inner tranquility.

This exercise contains within it not only the wisdom of
our relationship to the spiritual world, but also the preparation needed to experience what we are required to develop
so that we may carry this into and illuminate the spiritual
world from within our own hearts. We practice inner exercises not with an expectation of personal achievement, but
with a willingness to be transformed and a willingness to
learn of the ways of divine love.

The Sun Never Says
—Hafiz

Even
after
all this time
the sun never says to the earth,
"You owe me"

Look
what happens
with a love like that –

it lights the whole
world.[17]

For the esotericist and for the meditant, entering into a relationship with the spiritual world while carrying personal expectation creates a block to the in-streaming forces; this is simply because the personal element is present, and it acts as a block.

Of course, when an entrance to the spiritual world is induced through substance use, then the individual is not blocked, because the chemicals have formed the bridge for them by means of the doorways of the body and therefore one enters without fulfilling the requirements that would be necessary in order to maintain inner freedom. This can now become another dependency for individuals, on account of the ease with which one enters the spiritual world through the substance's ability to override the conditions required by the spiritual world for today's initiation. When the substance can do it for you, you yourself, your personal element, no longer stands in the way as a block; but if you have to do it yourself, then each time you meditate you are faced with the task of reorganizing your inner world, which requires turning away from your personal self and giving all of your capacity to this relationship with the divine. Anything we receive through that relationship will have been bridged solely on account of our efforts, but simultaneously a matter of grace from the divine spiritual world; the spiritual world gives us, in response to these efforts, exactly what we need for our progress.

Often people hold consciousness-altering substances in high regard because they are held in high regard by ancient cultures; and in a certain sense, as we become world citizens we learn more and more about each other and our cultural practices. This can be incredibly beneficial to humanity's progress, especially in light of the cultural "whitewashing" and "gentrification" that is so prevalent. Western minds are waking up to the recognition that one culture does not hold the whole picture. However, through the eyes of evolving consciousness, we have to be able to recognize that our technological advancements have changed us, that this has had consequences for our interior life, and that it has severely affected our bodily constitution.

We can most readily see this in how the industrial revolution and the enhancement of technology and all that consequently benefitted us has had such a tremendous impact on our inner world. We first developed technologies that took the place of what we had to do with our own will forces. This gave us the machines that alleviated us from being bound to using our will forces for basic survival. It is said that in order to function, the average Western home would now require the physical power of 23 people if we were forced to carry out with our own will forces all of the services that our technology currently does for us. A recent study showed how the Amish people have superior metabolic health, as they have not converted to technology in order to replace the efforts of their own will. Their will is constantly engaged in non-motorized activity, bringing improved metabolic health.

These advancements in technology have also allowed us to freely choose our work. It began liberating us from a survival mentality, and enabled us to enter one of enrichment and education. Just consider the so-called "free time," or recreational time, that we have as a result of industrialization. But also consider what people do with this time. It is extraordinary to see what gifts of liberation machine technology has bestowed upon humanity, and yet with that free time we have generally brought the nature of technology into our interior worlds and thereby stunted our use of our will forces.

We can see the further effects of this at work as we proceeded to develop the technology that took over the necessity for our feeling-experiencing to be engaged in the tasks at hand. All the advancements in medicine and science, all the machines for sensing and experiencing, such as blood pressure machines, or the thermometer to read temperature, have replaced our earlier reliance on the human feeling-experience of sensing into the illness processes of the patient. Now the laboratory takes over the assessment that earlier would have required the inner being of the physician. Today, the detective cannot get a search warrant based on a hunch. The systems of the "feeling technology" have taken over that task, and we have created laws to uphold these systems.

The diagnosis arises from the technology of feeling – in this case, the forensic science. At this point, we also built the technologies of entertainment, television, radio, etc. We did not take the liberated feeling and school it, but rather we put it on the couch. Sitting back on the couch, the technology of the screen not only provides us with what to think and feel, but amplifies the sensory and feeling stimuli in such a way that blunts our refined feeling system. For example, only a generation ago the news would not have shown people being massacred, but now we watch real people actually being murdered on a regular basis. Consider how our feelings are now liberated for other things, such as the internal and external exploration of experiences in the world and in the arts, in relationships and community life. However, the instrument of feeling is blunted by the same technology that could liberate us from being bound to having to use our feeling in a certain direction. Also consider how we now utilize the feeling world to stay within the comfort zone of experiences that are known and preferred. How we squander feeling-time in front of one movie or another and how young people push the feeling-boundaries with horror, self-harm, and substances in order to feel more.

And now we have built the technologies to do our thinking for us: the computers. In one way, this has also, like the other technologies, potentially liberated human beings from the mundane intellectual thinking world. The computers can do the brain thinking, and they do it better than we can. We are therefore free to utilize our thinking in ways computers cannot, such as imaginative thinking. If we let the computers fulfill the mundane thinking activities, then we could have more time to expand our thinking capacity. Instead, we are generally giving our time back to the machine and building a computer network, the "internet of things," that will keep us connected via machine rather than liberate our time for deepening community life and human relationships.

Consider the growing realms of thinking that we have available to us, such as online study and all the knowledge at our fingertips that we are exposed to and that present us with so many points of view. Also consider how computers and the internet are now being designed in such a way that you are encouraged to see things more from your own point of view, so that you are streamed into thoughts that validate what you already think.

In one way or another, each of these technologies have had a positive, progressive effect on the potential liberation of the human being in the capacity to freely use their will, thinking, and feeling. On the other hand, they have had a negative impact on the human being because this freed thinking, feeling, and willing has been bound back to the machine, and is causing the amplification of the industrialized interior world that we now bear. In this way, our own thinking, feeling, and willing is blunted, under-utilized, diminished. This relationship to the industrial technological revolution outside us is an image of the internal industrial change of the past that is now determining the growth of the world.

A human being today who has been internally changed through the industrial revolution has a different interior resource and soul-scape than those who have managed to maintain an interior world unpolluted by the external industrial revolution. According to our inner resources, we create differently.

This new inner world is being passed on by heredity that, since the industrial age, has vastly changed the starting point of esoteric schooling for these peoples. We have lost our natural relationship to the spirit and although we may have gained greater personal freedom, what has happened to our spiritual growth? With that personal freedom, we have advanced, but we have also diminished, raped, and pillaged other cultures. The industrialized interior world of each individual needs to rebuild, out of freedom, an individualized relationship to the spiritual world, which it can no longer achieve un-freely because it cannot go backwards. We cannot return to the old wisdom from out of this new interior and exterior constitution. We have to take this constitution forward, and this constitution has become so individualized that it insists upon an individualized relationship to the spirit.

This is not the same for the indigenous cultures that still live in harmony with the natural world around them. Their constitution has not been distorted by an internal industrialization of their being and of the way they think and feel about their relationship to spirit and to earth. The starting point for their connection with the spirit is vastly different from that of the people of the industrialized interiority. We can see this by exploring the conditions of esoteric training that are given from out of the modern esoteric schooling through Rudolf Steiner. As we read through each one of these conditions, while keeping in mind our knowledge of the indigenous cultures, we may be able to recognize this for ourselves.

We can see what it takes for a human being to live life in accordance with these conditions when that individual is separated from the realities of the spiritual world. Attempting to fulfill these conditions is a practice in and of itself. If we have had the privilege to be exposed to the ways of being and doing cultivated in these ancient cultures and with these indigenous peoples, then we will see that the training that must be given to the industrialized interiority is already a way of life for them, a natural principle of life. So although Rudolf Steiner has looked at each of these from the point of view of the separated self, we can also see how these conditions are innate and therefore not in need of practice and cultivation in the indigenous peoples of the world who have not been affected in their interior lives by industrialization; yet, these conditions are a necessity for the person of today with an industrialized interior life.

Exercise: take these conditions and contemplate how easy it is for you to live according to them on a daily basis, without effort. It becomes evident that for the industrialized people, these conditions require a sustained effort or we easily resort to forgetting them.

1. The first condition is that the student should pay heed to the advancement of bodily and spiritual health. Of course, health does not depend, in the first instance, upon the individual; but the effort to improve in this respect lies within the scope of all. Sound knowledge can alone proceed from sound human beings. The unhealthy are not rejected, but it is demanded of the student that they should have the will to lead a healthy life. In this respect they must attain the greatest possible independence. The good counsels of others, freely bestowed, though generally

*unsought, are as a rule superfluous. Each must endeavor
to take care of themselves. From the physical aspect it will
be more a question of warding off harmful influences than
of anything else. In fulfilling our duties, we must often do
things that are detrimental to our health. We must decide
at the right moment to place duty higher than the care of
our health. But just think how much can be avoided with
a little good will. Duty must in many cases stand higher
than health, often, even, than life itself; but pleasure must
never stand higher, as far as the student is concerned.
For them pleasure can only be a means to health and to
life, and in this connection we must, above all, be honest
and truthful with ourselves. There is no use in leading an
ascetic life when the underlying motive is the same in this
case as in other enjoyments. Some may derive satisfaction from asceticism just as others can from wine-bibbing,
but they must not imagine that this sort of asceticism will
assist them in attaining higher knowledge. Many ascribe
to their circumstances everything which apparently prevents them from making progress. They say they cannot
develop themselves under their conditions of life. Now,
many may find it desirable for other reasons to change
their conditions of life, but no one need do so for the
purpose of esoteric training. For the latter, a person need
only do as much as possible, whatever their position, to
further the health of body and soul. Every kind of work
can serve the whole of humanity; and it is a surer sign of
greatness of soul to perceive clearly how necessary for this
whole is a petty, perhaps even an offensive employment
than to think: "This work is not good enough for me;*

*I am destined for something better." Of special impor-
tance for the student is the striving for complete health
of mind. An unhealthy life of thought and feeling will not
fail to obstruct the path to higher knowledge. Clear, calm
thinking, with stability of feeling and emotion, form here
the basis of all work. Nothing should be further removed
from the student than an inclination toward a fantasti-
cal, excitable life, toward nervousness, exaggeration, and
fanaticism. They should acquire a healthy outlook on all
circumstances of life; they should meet the demands of life
with steady assurance, quietly letting all things make their
impression on them and reveal their message. They should
be at pains to do justice to life on every occasion. All one-
sided and extravagant tendencies in their sentiments and
criticisms should be avoided. Failing this, they would find
their way merely into worlds of their own imagination,
instead of higher worlds; in place of truth, their own pet
opinions would assert themselves. It is better for the student to be matter-of-fact, than excitable and fantastic.*[18]

With the industrialized interiority, as a group, we eat
primarily for pleasure, and only secondarily for health.
How else can fast food exist? We waste food. We commodify things that support the advancement of bodily and
spiritual health, and in their commodification we have
already destroyed the condition. We commodify lifestyles,
ways of eating, and spiritual practices, which would be
impossible in cultures unaffected by industrialization.
However, these cultures that have been distorted by the
industrialized age are now struggling to maintain their

own physical and spiritual health, as the so-called modern tendencies impinge upon them, and they will soon be further impinged upon by the reality of the next revelation of industrialization: the computerized world.

2. *The second condition is that the student should feel themselves coordinated as a link in the whole of life. Much iş included in the fulfillment of this condition, but each can only fulfill it in their own manner. If I am a teacher, and my pupil does not fulfill my expectations, I must not divert my resentment against him but against myself. I must feel myself as one with my pupil, to the extent of asking myself: "Is my pupil's deficiency not the result of my own action?" Instead of directing my feelings against them I shall rather reflect on my own attitude, so that the pupil may in the future be better able to satisfy my demands. Proceeding from such an attitude, a change will come over the student's whole way of thinking. This holds good in all things, great or small. Such an attitude of mind, for instance, alters the way I regard a criminal. I suspend my judgment and say to myself: "I am, like them, only a human being. Through favorable circumstances I received an education which perhaps alone saved me from a similar fate." I may then also come to the conclusion that this human brother or sister of mine would have become a different person had my teachers taken the same pains with them as they took with me. I shall reflect on the fact that something was given to me which was withheld from them, that I enjoy my fortune precisely because it was denied them. And then I shall naturally come to think of*

myself as a link in the whole of humanity and a sharer in the responsibility for everything that occurs. This does not imply that such a thought should be immediately translated into external acts of agitation. It should be cherished in stillness within the soul. Then quite gradually it will set its mark on the outward demeanor of the student. In such matters each can only begin by reforming themselves. It is of no avail, in the sense of the foregoing thoughts, to make general demands on the whole of humanity. It is easy to decide what people ought to be; but the student works in the depths, not on the surface. It would therefore be quite wrong to relate the demand here indicated with external, least of all political, demands; with such matters this training can have nothing to do. Political agitators know, as a rule, what to demand of other people; but they say little of demands on themselves.[19]

Our ability to live with this condition takes a lot of practice for the inner industrialized human being, and yet for the indigenous cultures this condition is second nature. Even the land itself is united and one with the consciousness of the group. Society operates in a state of relatedness. Everything and everyone is related. There is real belief that people, objects, and the environment are all connected.

3. This brings us to the third condition. The student must work his way upward to the realization that their thoughts and feelings are as important for the world as their actions. It must be realized that it is equally injurious to hate a fellow-being as to strike them. The realization will then follow that by perfecting ourselves we accomplish something not only for ourselves, but for the whole world. The world derives equal benefit from our untainted feelings and thoughts as from our good demeanor, and as long as we cannot believe in this cosmic importance of our inner life, we are unfit for the path that is here described. We are only filled with the right faith in the significance of our inner self, of our soul, when we work at it as though it were at least as real as all external things. We must admit that our every feeling produces an effect, just as does every action of our hand.[20]

This third condition again is a natural condition for many indigenous peoples. The notion that "thoughts are things" is held to be true not only in esoteric knowledge; this is a matter of general understanding in many indigenous cultures, although it is expressed in a different way. Continue to contemplate the next conditions and how they are already a practice for the industrialized interior peoples and a natural way of being for those unaffected by the industrialized world.

4. *The fourth condition: to acquire the conviction that the real essence of the human being does not lie in his exterior but in his interior. Anyone regarding themselves as a product of the outer world, as a result of the physical world, cannot succeed in this esoteric training, for the feeling that we are beings of soul and spirit forms its very basis. The acquisition of this feeling renders the student fit to distinguish between inner duty and outward success. They learn that the one cannot be directly measured by the other. They must find the proper mean between what is*

indicated by external conditions and what they recognize as the right conduct for themselves. They should not force upon their environment anything for which it can have no understanding, but also they must be quite free from the desire to do only what can be appreciated by those around them. The voice of their own soul struggling honestly toward knowledge must bring them the one and only recognition of the truths for which they stand. But they must learn as much as they possibly can from their environment so as to discover what those around them need, and what is good for them. In this way they will develop within themselves what is known in spiritual science as the "spiritual balance." An open heart for the needs of the outer world lies on one of the scales, and inner fortitude and unfaltering endurance on the other.[21]

5. This brings us to the fifth condition: steadfastness in carrying out a resolution. Nothing should induce the student to deviate from a resolution they may have taken, save only the perception that they were in error. Every resolution is a force, and if this force does not produce an immediate effect at the point to which it was applied, it nevertheless works on in its own way. Success is only decisive when an action arises from desire. But all actions arising from desire are worthless in relation to the higher worlds. There, love for an action is alone the decisive factor. In this love, every impulse that impels the student to action should fulfill itself. Undismayed by failure, they will never grow weary of endeavoring repeatedly to translate some resolution into action. And in this way they reach the stage of not waiting to see the outward effect of their actions, but of contenting themselves with performing them. They will learn to sacrifice their actions, even their whole being, to the world, however the world may receive their sacrifice. Readiness for a sacrifice, for an offering such as this, must be shown by all who would pursue the path of esoteric training.[22]

6. A sixth condition is the development of a feeling of thankfulness for everything with which the human being is favored. We must realize that our existence is a gift from the entire universe. How much is needed to enable each one of us to receive and maintain his existence! How much do we not owe to nature and to our fellow human beings! Thoughts such as these must come naturally to all who seek esoteric training, for if the latter do not feel inclined to entertain them, they will be incapable of developing within themselves that all-embracing love which is necessary for the attainment of higher knowledge. Nothing can reveal itself to us which we do not love. And every revelation must fill us with thankfulness, for we ourselves are the richer for it.[23]

7. All these conditions must be united in a seventh: to regard life unceasingly in the manner demanded by these conditions. The student thus makes it possible to give their life the stamp of uniformity. All their modes of expression will, in this way, be brought into harmony, and no longer contradict each other. And thus they will prepare themselves for the inner tranquility they must attain during the preliminary steps of their training.[24]

The physical constitutional starting point of the inner life, which affects the harmony between body, soul, and spirit, is very different for those who are held by, and who are working through, their generational heredity in indigenous cultures than it is for human beings who are industrialized inwardly through their heredity, as has now become the case for a majority of the Western generations. This separated consciousness has to repair the bridge between the spirit and the earth. This bridge in the external world is called the biosphere. But if the bridge is not developed internally, then in the context of our work in the biosphere, our genuine biosphere consciousness will not succeed and the planet itself will enter into the sixth mass-extinction phase.

We need a dramatic change in how we work in the outer world in order to protect the biosphere. In the inner industrialized world of the individual, we also need a dramatic change. In the esoteric schooling, physical earth represents one aspect of spiritual consciousness and the biosphere represents another aspect. Sometimes this is called the astral world. It is where we interchange thoughts. We are interconnected in the astral world; we are already a collective community. If we are unable to make the necessary transition and bring our spiritual bridge-building into the future, we will be unable to maintain the external biosphere and the earth will suffer exponentially. One of the greatest temptations is to bring into this endeavor the corporate form, which has corrupted economics and has brought increased profits to only a few. Instead of perpetuating outdated methods bound to greed and accumulation for the few into the next evolutionary phase, a sharing economy is essential, as this is the nature of the biosphere.

We have ripped out of the body of the earth so many of its resources and polluted its being; we cannot think for a moment that our personal bodily inheritance is separate from that. Just as it is needed for the healthy growth of the human being, the earth now needs to be supported in an intensified way with the cosmic stream that brings about its health and wellbeing. We need to establish a life-giving connection between the cosmic forces and the earth.

These healthy, life-giving connections were natural to the inner life in the past. Human beings were conscious of the spiritual world, which gave meaning and understanding to life; the natural world was a source of nourishment, harmony, and balance, and the arts and cultural life imbued life with relationship and experience. We have neglected to care for all three resources in the world. We are therefore called to reestablish in freedom a new care for these necessary, life-sustaining resources. We are called to cultivate a new and quickened connection to the natural world, the arts, and the spirit, now and into the future, if we are to prevent our demise. Reestablishing and building a new relationship between ourselves and the natural world, the arts, and the spirit is the only way to maintain inner health. There are many practical ways in which we can do this new bridging.

Practices such as biodynamic farming offer a way of doing this for the natural world and the human being. It not only seeks to heal the earth by replenishing the soils, but it also rebuilds a harmonious relationship between human beings and the kingdoms of nature. It seeks to establish a living example of the creative relationship that is possible between the human being and the natural kingdoms. It reaches beyond where we are now into the future through supporting the bridge between cosmic forces and the earth.

The biosphere of the world is a whole, and therefore what we have done in one part of the world affects other parts; we would not be considering the necessity of applying biodynamic preparations to parts of the Amazon just based on soil rejuvenation. However, because biodynamics works as a bridge between cosmic and earthly forces, it also has an effect on the biosphere. Organic farming, which serves the earth by not implanting into it everything that is being created from the extraction of fossil fuel – all the pesticides and chemicals – cannot build cosmic forces through the bridge to the biosphere in the way biodynamic farming can. We not only need to avoid creating further imbalances in the kingdoms of nature through our negative impact, but also to participate in healing and renewing our relationship to them.

We do need biodynamic farming in those parts of the world where industrialization has harmed the nature kingdoms, where the soil has been depleted, where the harmony of nature has been disordered, and the healthy connection between the heavens and the earth has been destroyed through our lack of care and understanding for the other kingdoms that serve the world. Biodynamic farming works not only on transforming the past, but also on regenerating into the future. It has a future mission for the biosphere of the planet.

Our body is our own piece of land, and like any piece of land it cannot be separated from the whole. Unfortunately, this industrialized body requires a different form of support in order to regain health. We can see differences between industrialized peoples and the indigenous tribes, whose intestinal flora is far superior to what now exists in the newborn child of the industrialized world. We have inherited bodies that are a reflection of what we have done to the body of the earth.

When we use a physical substance to induce an altered state of consciousness, we are in fact using the bridge of the body to reach toward spiritual activity. And the affected industrialized body – not through diet, but through its very heredity – does not have the same health and organizing structures that exist in the spiritual-physical conditions of the indigenous peoples, who are born into healthy indigenous systems that have not been overly influenced by the corrupting forces of an internally industrialized society.

However, again, we cannot go backwards, and we need to be where we are. No matter how often we fast or pack our bags and live with tribes in the Andes, we have been born into a stream that bears the weight of its ancestors. And it is up to every individual to take the next healthy step of progression forward within the stream into which they are born.

Taking psychedelics is very different for the internally industrialized human being than it is for someone unaffected by industrialized interiority. It will be different to yet a further degree for the future computerized being that is developing now. If you attempt to wring out wisdom from the industrialized body, it will be distorted because it bears the consequences of what we have done to the earth. However, the path forward for those born to this internalized industrial world is an arduous and long path because of everything that must be corrected and brought back into harmony on account of the internal repercussions of what we have done to the outer world.

The responsibility to begin by correcting this separation is not an impossible task because we are indeed supported by the spiritual strength to do this. And that is why we stand in a time where we as individuals have a capacity, out of ourselves, to individually start the work of correcting the collective error of the internal industrial impact upon the health of the world. The people of the industrialized interior cannot impose the same mistake upon other cultures as they have done in the past. They cannot place upon the other their own healing path. The pathways that can lead a particular culture forward must be found by the people of this culture themselves. These pathways may be different from those of other cultures, as we are responsible in different ways for human progress. Just as, in our present age, it is impossible for someone else to carry out your inner development path for you, so it is also impossible for one culture or group to impose development upon another culture or group in the sense of what path of evolution and development they should take. A culture's future development must come from within, and not through being applied from without. Therefore, the industrialized interior peoples must simply take responsibility for their own errors, but they cannot assume that this is also the way forward for other cultures that are not of the same interiority; indigenous cultures or others may embrace their own respective responsibilities out of their own respective insights.

However, the industrialized people can be immensely grateful to those groups that have held off the onslaught of the negative aspects of the internalized industrial consciousness, thereby allowing the world to still have insights into the possibility of working together once again in harmony with the natural kingdoms of the world. These groups have maintained the wisdom of the relationship between humanity and the land against the odds of the industrialized age and we can learn from each other's capacities as well as mistakes.

It is time to utilize all the freed thinking, feeling, will forces that industrialization has afforded us and direct them toward the great work of inner evolution so that we can undo the effects of the industrialized interiority and the harm that this has brought upon the external world. We and the world are ready for us to develop new capacities with the time we have left. What are we doing with our so-called "free time"? Are we able to actively progress the human inner life through our own efforts and in this way offer the next generations a world that is sustaining to their inner life, in turn allowing them the possibility of creating a better future for all?

Through the arts and the cultural life, we can perceive how creativity, in all the forms available to us, is a great potential means for all these freed forces to think creatively into a better future for humanity and to feel and experience the world in such a way that the world and the individual meet in depth, giving rise to something new from out of this unique meeting. Creativity gives us the potential to bring this new inner experience into the world in order to enrich the inner life of others. Creating through what we do, in whatever the task before us may be, becomes an act of creating anew even if it is a matter of uniting with and building upon a creative process that has already been given an expression in the world. For each individual may add something new to, or illuminate in a new way, what they have come to know and love.

Below is a piece of work by an artistic colleague who has worked extensively with the legend of Parzival and who, through this work, has been able to continue the creative process further. The arts are not only another healing path for the industrialized interior, but they serve as a preventative measure for additional harm, as they help us to maintain the inner capacities of the child and to awaken an internal sensitivity to the external and internal worlds. For all art serves to enrich the inner life. This piece is chosen because it speaks, in its inner language, to what has also been expressed in this book.

> There is a love that hovers o're our souls,
> Like wings of angels poised upon a breath,
> Awaiting recognition from our eyes.
> For when, within each other's gaze we see

The stars alight and feel the warming band,
Uniting in a sunlit ring of grace -
Like home forgotten but returned anew
Within a waking moment like a dream -
Then masters of winged servants weave above
Our heads and 'round our wavering hearts begin
To form a vessel, fortified with strength
And courage transcending earthly means, to catch
A drop of wisdom's light, from far beyond
The reaches, which may fall into our cup.
And nothing of this world or of the next
Can breach its solid rim or shake its base -
This sturdy vessel linked betwixt the lives
Of all who see their part and hold their piece
Within the chain of spirit bridging worlds:
Strong enough to stand through any siege,
Light enough t'illume the darkest night,
And warm enough to thaw the coldest heart.
And through this causeway built between our souls,
As though from heaven itself, pours alchemy -
A fiery liquid gold - into the world,
Which burns away impurities and lifts
Our eyes up to the heights, as though the sun
Had given each of us one of its rays
To carry through the world.
So was the love
That hovered o'er two noble souls who lived.
Between their royal hearts a third ideal
Was born in purity and innocence,
Perfected in potential. Had they been
Inhabitants of heaven, it would have stayed
A shimmering perfection, unrealized;
A bright and hopeful promise, unsullied
By pangs and longings of this world's constraints.
A love like that is not a thing of earth.
Yet, born into this world, accompanied
By labor's cries and given for no gain,
It may be freed. Thus love fulfills its aim

And so begins the struggle and the pain.
So Parzival and Condwiramurs his queen,
Were crowned with grace yet set before the trial,
Of testing life, for all whose hearts seek truth.[25]

Whatever we meet in our tasks, we can unite ourselves with its inner activity and through our effort bring it into life in a newly creative process. We all can give something toward this future, whether that be through our inner spiritual life that expresses itself in the way we individually live in the world, through the arts and cultural life that express our relationships to each other, or through our activity of living in harmony with the natural kingdoms, which expresses our reverence for the world. We all have a place in this becoming of humanity into its next evolutionary phase, which we may participate in through our creative activity. We can creatively transform the industrialized interior world through a wisdom-filled spiritual life, through experiencing the arts and participating in their effects, as well as through our efforts to live in harmony with the kingdoms of nature and our surrounding natural world. Each of us can make creative progress in one or more directions; and as we do so, we support the progress of all.

3

A Bridge to the Future

MEDITATION DERIVES FROM the word *medi*, meaning middle, and meditation means participating in the middle. Meditation opens the portals, through the inner development of the human being, to the sun path of spiritual consciousness. The sun path initiates us; on this path, we develop capacities that will be needed by all people in order to progress in the times ahead. There are many steps or doorways in our spiritual growth, just as there are in our physical growth. These steps or stages of spiritual development are sometimes called "degrees" in our initiation; and in various traditions, the essential nature of the first three degrees have become open knowledge in recent times. In physical development, the young child learns to walk, talk, and think. In spiritual development, we also acquire the necessary stages of growth.

The first degree of our inner relationship to the sun path is the archetype of the acquisition of self-knowledge and the evolution of our consciousness, and it results in the understanding of humanity's evolution of consciousness, with which we are intimately linked, as we have played a part in it through our own participation. The second degree develops our capacity to learn a new language for new realms by understanding the wisdom and harmony that are the fabric of the divine spiritual world. This also deepens our direct understanding of the relationship of the divine toward the diverting spiritual forces, as well as the effect of these forces upon the human psyche and the external world. The third degree is the rebirth into conscious spiritual life. It means that the student can stand and assess the events of life from the eyes of spiritual perception; it is the beginning of a life in consciousness in which one does not require the sense world in order to be aware. The student is now born into spiritual life, awakened from the slumber of the sense world. The spiritual world is now a living reality for the individual; they can now begin a new life, one which renews all of life for them.

Each step of inner initiation marks a new aspect of our inner development that will take time to awaken. This is because, in most cases, we need to learn the necessary precautions and to be able to assimilate all that these new vistas will reveal. Even though these steps can be revealed openly to the world, they must be awakened and assimilated internally by each and every individual themselves if they are to produce the transformative change that can be sustainable and solid in all aspects of being.

Genuine initiation awakens the next evolutionary step in an individual, a step that will be awakened by the many in the future. Humanity has already proceeded through many evolutionary steps in consciousness and each of these steps has first been awakened by the initiates; they were the first to take hold of these new developmental steps and in turn steer the outer world in the corresponding direction. Today, many more individuals are consciously involved with this process, and the necessity for humanity's survival and growth requires that it be this way.

Individual initiation reveals the first significant changes that will later become a collective capacity for the whole of humanity. Initiation cultivates the next states of consciousness that humanity as a whole has the potential to awaken to eventually. When this awakening begins for the individual, they can recognize how the inner development path is the initiation process not only for the individual alone, but also for the wider world. Rudolf Steiner describes the new capacity awaiting our development in terms of three unfolding components: first, imaginative consciousness, then inspirational consciousness, and third, intuitive consciousness.

Developing these three new capacities has been given through the initiation school as the primary pathway for the people of the industrialized interiority. Having these capacities allows us to see what lives and weaves behind the manifest world. Through imaginative consciousness, which in this sense has nothing to do with making things up or having a personal kaleidoscope, imagination gives us an internal picture-perception of what exists behind the manifest sense world. Rudolf Steiner presented many exercises on how to awaken this capacity in his book, *Knowledge of the Higher Worlds and Its Attainment*. To perceive inwardly in picture form what lives spiritually behind the outer reality of things could be termed a "reverse ritual." Outer ritual is commonly understood as an external, visual expression of the realities of the spiritual world, while the reverse ritual is to lift up our capacities so that they may become conscious of the spiritual realties that are invisible to the senses.

All peoples throughout the world have developed outer rituals and ceremonies of various kinds in order to outwardly express their particular connection to the realms of spirit. True outer rituals are enactments of various spiritual realities that exist. A ritual of this kind makes visual, experiential, and participatory within the sense world the spiritual realities that exist within the realms of spirit. Ritual brings spiritual realties into perceptible manifestation and in doing so draws upon the consciousnesses that exist in spiritual realms to engage right then and there in the enactment. This is done by presenting the sequence of signs and symbols (a language following the law of correspondences) corresponding to the spiritual realties or events that the ritual is intended to reenact. The rituals of humanity's transformative evolutionary events, and also the individual events of evolving through the degrees, exist in a living way on another plane of existence, but are expressed outwardly within the external ritual according to the culture that the particular ritual is serving.

Today, many seekers of the spirit are attracted to participating in various forms of ritual, especially in the context of ingesting consciousness-altering substances that have been a part of ritual practice in the customs of First Nation peoples. Ritual has been a supportive doorway to an inner experience of spiritual realities; and yet, we are now capable of awakening this experience within our inner world through the path of meditation without the necessity of outwardly manifested forms.

For the industrialized people, initiation today does not require the outer form of ritual; but many find the outer event to be a break in normal daily life that serves to focus the inner attention toward the spirit. In accordance with present-day human development, the initiation steps for the industrialized people would be pathways to cultivating an inner connection through raising our individual consciousness to the plane of spiritual reality, where these realities live and can be engaged with as a direct inner experience. In this way, we could say that the people of the industrialized interiority are learning how to create the "reverse ritual" within the next step in their initiation.

To "see" with imaginative consciousness would be to perceive inwardly the spiritual reality behind the appearance of things. To have attained inspirational consciousness would be to be able to "read," to gain the meaning of what those pictures are conveying, to be able to hear what is being communicated in those realms. To have attained intuitive consciousness would be to have the capacity to unite oneself with what is present spiritually in such a way that you are a full participant in this realm: to be a participant within the realities of spiritual revelation so that they are a part of your knowledge, a knowledge and accompanying strength that you cannot be separated from. Even in the spiritual world, knowledge is power, but not one that can be used for self-gain without dire consequences.

When an individual can perceive for themselves the world of spirit behind the manifest sense world, they are also able to see the world of spirit that is not presently manifest as a sensory impression. When this develops even to the smallest degree, that individual then knows themselves to be a citizen of the spiritual world and at this point all loneliness, all sense of being a separated, isolated being, leaves.

In today's external world, this wisdom of the degrees of inner development is revealed in various ways; however, this is not always understood, even when this wisdom is enacted in the form of a full externalized ritual, as is the case in some traditions, such as the Freemasons. There are various levels of knowledge held by those participating in and enacting the rituals, and this will affect the ability of the ritual to bring forth the wisdom revealed in it as well as the observer's ability to read this wisdom. However, the wisdom lives in the great rituals even if we cannot read it; these rituals are also enacted in many different religious services. The capacity to fully grasp the language and meaning of the great rituals can only be developed through interior development culminating in participating in the second degree. In fact, it could be said that in today's consciousness, according to prior understanding, participating in external rituals has very different effects and very little effect unless there is some preparation and understanding. The same can be said of all our external experiences, which we receive in different ways according to our inner preparation. Two people could be exposed to the same experience, such as sleeping under a starlit sky; one may feel deeply moved by it and will carry that impression with them, whereas for the other it makes no difference to their inner lives. Our internal world allows the external world to take effect in us, to penetrate us, and to have an impact in different ways.

However ready we may be, understanding the symbols of the external rituals can be a useful tool for us to prepare ourselves for the experiences that we will need to encounter in our inner development, which is the only true place of transformation. However, by understanding what lies within these rituals, we are able to see that within the outer ritual lies the possibility of bringing alignment to the individuals present in order to quicken their progress on the inner path. But for most people today, study and understanding is the necessary preparation that will allow the ritual knowledge to take an inner effect.

The initiation rituals of inner development focus on individual transformation and the events that will come to pass. The religious rituals focus on the world's transformation and the events that have been. However, these two unite in spiritual ritual because "what was" and "what is becoming" exist simultaneously in the living present moment of "what is" in the living spiritual world.

In exploring their meaning through understanding, the outer initiation rituals of the three degrees provide another way for us to gain some insights into what actually takes place in the inner initiation of the individual. For those who are highly intellectual, any knowledge imparted through the ritual symbols can become another block to inner perception because the intellect thinks it can cognize all and that this cognizing is enough, when, in fact, the intellect's cognizing something is not the initiation. The intellect needing to "know it" can be the interference that can block the wisdom of the ritual form working inwardly as inner representation. It would be like listening to a fairy tale with an academic ear for the history contained in it. The picture-forming nature of the fairy tales is what serves the child, not the intellectual evaluation of what the picture means in history. There is a certainty and knowing that the outer ritual is not the degree itself, but only another potential preparation for it; and that preparation depends on whether it can be entered into in the right frame of mind.

The ritual is therefore a rich language of symbols, each signifying something to the inner development and relating to what will be encountered therein. And it is in this light that it is useful to explore and understand the rituals: not to encourage outer ritual work, but rather to recognize the meaning of such rituals in the inner path. Some rituals are the enactment of spiritual events that have changed the course of history, and according to the stream, religion, lodge, or society, they may vary greatly depending on what parts of the greater spiritual cosmic events of which they are an expression are being enacted. Many schools also express these symbols differently, and therefore it is not unusual to first have some education and esoteric study around the meaning of the symbols with which you are participating. The rituals of the degrees outwardly express the individual inner initiation path, which itself does not require outer ritual but rather inner transformation.

The study and content of any given ritual is generally well-formed, even exact. This is also the way it is with most meditative exercises of a particular society or stream. This is primarily for the purpose of producing the results of awakening that prepare the individual for what they will meet, whether that be their own higher 'I' or inner guide, or the next stage of their inner development. But in our industrialized interiority, many people have taken our global access to the external world as a way of seeking self-development. This can be both a benefit and a hindrance to making progress.

In the past, most people found their right stream or, more likely, they were born into it. They then followed a pathway that was laid out before them, a pathway that others in the stream had walked before them. The instructions were like a map of a highly equipped mountain climber. If you do such and such, in such and such a way, then one day you yourself will get to the top. The guru or head of the tradition revealed how God was to be experienced and gave the conditions or rules that, if cultivated within yourself, would lead you to experience the divine.

More and more, we see a widening of our ability not only to accept other faiths or ways of development but also to participate in multiple traditions or pathways at once.

This global tendency has both benefits and hindrances. It can lead to an eclectic path that does not progress but keeps the individual engaged in spiritual "window-shopping," or it can lead to going from one technique to another, and thereby not deepening or moving beyond the preliminary steps of any path. On the other hand, it can also lead to finding common threads from the various paths that, when woven together, produce a stronger rope and certainty of foothold. It can produce a clarity through the interfacing of many modalities that, united as a whole, becomes clearer, producing a steady onward progression.

The great difference in terms of the effects on one person in contrast to another is determined by where you are in your own inner development. From the outset, what you do with the learning you acquire is dependent on the starting point. If someone already has a foothold in the second degree, then a multidisciplinary path can be of value in continuing to inform that degree. If, however, that is not the case and the student is at an earlier stage of inner expansion, then it is more likely to be a distraction from producing results of certainty, and a commitment to a single path may be more beneficial.

We stand in an unusual place in the evolution of our inner life. Never before have we seen the spiritual freedom of having so many options of various paths offered to the human being. Never before has this path felt so fully in our own hands to choose or to discard. At the same time, we need to be more aware of the consequences of our choices, as we are the guardians of our own path.

The industrialized interiority has produced many blocks to our capacity to inwardly acknowledge the realities of the spiritual world. The intellect needs to be convinced that the way is even worth walking. But for those who recognize the path, the industrialized interiority has yet other hindrances. We can become "inner path consumers" and impose the industrialized external approach to life upon the self-development path. It is necessary for us to learn not only the truth of spiritual realties, but also the *way* in which they are healthily revealed. This is a part of the schooling of today; it is needed in our time for the people of the industrialized interiority, since much of the industrialized ways of being have now been integrated internally. We are not only dealing with obvious hindrances such as ambition and wanting to be seen, recognized, and rewarded for our inner work, but many other hindrances now come in the form of inner states that do not lead us forward: being consumers, wanting things to come easily or quickly, being self-oriented, doing things for personal gain, expecting personal reward for inner work, being result-oriented. The hindrances will need to be purified in order for us to walk a genuine path, and those hindrances that are not purified will delay us on our path.

Increasingly, we are seeing that those born into religious traditions have turned away or feel disconnected from the path of the inner practices that lead to growing their relationship to God, virtue, and immortality. With the added element of the need for autonomy within the industrialized interiority, the starting point is new. Therefore, the individual must determine for themselves which path they want to walk. But because this is the industrialized shift, the recognition that the collective need to awaken can only be achieved through the uniting power of love must simultaneously be the impulse for the individual's steps forward.

Below are some of the archetypal experiences upon the path that the individual is likely to encounter consciously if the certainty and capacity of the spiritual life is to be attained. However, they are not stated in such a way as to appeal to the intellectual life; rather, they are given as symbols that can be contemplated and considered, much as one would take in certain meditation exercises and utilize them in contemplation or internal absorption in order that they may work upon the self, preparing for the necessary changes that the inner life will encounter. Each meditation verse or mantra is wisdom that is imbued with the realities of the path into the spiritual world as well as with the power to affect our inner life and bring about the necessary adjustments – if we have the will to engage with its activity on a regular basis. (See *Living Inner Development*.)[25]

Understanding the way toward the spiritual world helps to disarm the intellect, and in order to assist with this, the archetypal symbols of the externalized rituals are utilized. There are many symbols given in various schools, as well as meditations and inner exercises, and until we have passed the third degree it would be better not to let our personal self dictate the spiritual content of our inner absorption. Our personal self does not know how to initiate us into higher realms. But we can, by utilizing the forms from one tradition or another, access where we are on our inner path and give language to where we have been. This can help greatly in our striving and self-education. Each step has multiple symbols that, when contemplated, reveal a greater understanding of the way. Below, only a few symbols are spoken about from one point of view, but each has its own message to the inner life and its own potency for the individual. They are extracted from the outer ritual work, which in itself can only present the pictures of the inner path for today's consciousness, but which are to be understood as inner activities and steps to be surmounted inwardly, and not as something to be done outwardly.

We will begin by exploring the pre-degree training: "entering the chamber of reflection." The chamber of reflection is entered before starting each of the degrees as well as before any major shift on the way. It is useful to come to know this internal space intimately so that you can be clear that you yourself have decided in freedom to take the step you are about to take. It is a part of the inner training and strengthening to be able to willingly enter this space daily.

In this first symbol, the individual enters into the chamber of reflection before attempting to enter the temple. In the external chamber of reflection, we go down into a small, dark chamber with only a few items: a mirror, a candle, a notebook, and perhaps a few things pertaining to the degree you are considering. This is the place of calm and serenity in which we can embark on an inner absorption of the schooling. This chamber that we enter into daily is not entered in order to flee from the external world, but to build the internal world. In the silencing of the exterior, the interior rises and so do the mysteries of our inner world. This is also the place where one contemplates one's own readiness for the degree one is about to enter. There may be symbols of that particular degree in this preparatory chamber, which can also be contemplated. But apart from the small light you take with you, there is no other light inside.

Although the inner state of contemplation or meditation that corresponds to the chamber of reflection has been entered into many times, if not daily, it is useful to note that at the onset of a new degree in the interior world, many will recognize that there is often an unsettled feeling or feeling of difficulty, perhaps a feeling of isolation, or even a feeling that I've lost my way, a feeling of uncertainty on the path. This is a common experience before a new step is taken. There is no interior step that we need to take that we already feel capable of taking. It feels beyond our grasp, or as if we don't have the strength to endure it. And therefore in this darkened chamber we must wait before we feel ready to embark on this next step. If we do not come to an answer before the candle burns out, then we clearly are not yet sufficiently prepared.

> Do only what comes from the truth of your heart, what the care of your thoughts leads you to, what the strength of your will has steeled you to do.[26]

This chamber corresponds to a meditative state of inner absorption. Today, we alone need to asses our readiness for the interior extension through the degrees, as our readiness will determine the results and the integration. If we are able to succeed in inner absorption in the chamber of reflection, then we may be ready to move onwards. This is described here by Rudolf Steiner as an interior event in a meditation exercise.

Through such contemplation – which must become a life habit, indeed a condition of life, just as breathing is a condition for the life of the body – one gathers together the forces of the soul and, in gathering, strengthens them. One must only succeed, during those periods of inner contemplation, in completely controlling oneself in such a way that neither outer sensory impressions nor any memories of them are able to tinge one's soul life. Likewise, all those memories of what one has experienced in ordinary life, of what gave the soul joy or pain, must be silent so that the soul is completely and solely devoted to *what one oneself has determined*. The forces for suprasensory knowledge grow in the right way *only* from what one has achieved through such periods of inner contemplation, the content and form of which one has oneself produced by mobilizing the power of one's own soul. It does not matter from where one has acquired the content of the contemplation. One may have received it from a person knowledgeable in this realm, or from spiritual-scientific literature. One must only be sure to make this content one's own inner experience, rather than allowing oneself to be prompted to undertake a contemplation only through what comes from one's own soul or through what one personally regards as the best content for a contemplation. The latter has very little force, because the soul feels related to it from the outset and so does not need to exert the necessary effort toward becoming one with it. *It is in these efforts*, and not in being united with the content of the contemplation as such, that the effective means for the development of suprasensory forces of knowledge lie.[27]

In order to be ready to enter the mystery center of the heart, we need to have the capacity for inner absorption as expressed above. Without this capacity, which expresses a mastery over the moon path, we will be unequipped to utilize the sun path revelations. Until we have some seed of development in the moon capacities, the inner absorption does not occur and we find our personal self in the chamber of reflection with us. We leave the chamber of reflection, our own minds, and proceed to the mystery center, the heart of the inner temple. Before entering the temple or interior of the lodge, the candidate removes from their body all personal items, jewelry, money, clothing – anything connected with the personal identity and the earthly world.

This is a symbol of the corresponding shift from filling the inner world with all that is personal to the faculties of the faithful observer, the experiencing-harmonizing capacity, and the individualized free will. These three themselves are activated with an internal gaze, even if they are only present in seed form. They are the preparation for the initial degree, but are further developed during the first degree itself and are even more fully present as the higher degrees unfold.

When the child is born into the sense world, they are cared for by the people and their surrounding environment in such a way as to awaken the seeds of the three essential capacities that are necessary for learning from life.

These three – *attention*, *attachment*, and *self-regulation* – are recognized as a birthright to the child. First they come to the child from without, from their caregivers, and are undisturbed by a supportive outer environment that does not create imbalances. As the child grows, they unfold these three essential capacities and eventually become independent learners within life. In the spiritual world, the three seeds of learning are the *faithful observer*, the *experiencing-harmonizing capacity*, and the *strengthened free will*. These three allow us to learn from the surrounding spiritual world, and also allow for the growth of a full and healthy inner devoplment through the learning we acquire.

With these three spiritual learning-seeds clearly activated, we can knock upon the door for entry. Today, each individual must knock for themselves, meaning the knock is one of the preparatory symbols of that degree. This symbol may be represented differently in each school, but it produces certain effects in our consciousness that are common to every school. Those who can knock are given permission to enter if they have achieved the right preparation. There is always a doorkeeper. When they are asked "who seeks to enter the degree?" The response required is, "a free person."

This "free person" is free in several ways; they are free as in "I come of my own volition," but also free of my personal striving and free of my automatic self. Anyone who has achieved some inner steps will understand the meaning of these symbols even if they belong to a tradition, schooling, or path that has no outer ritual, as inner development is an experience of liberation.

Three primary experiences of self-knowledge are unfolding within the first degree: 1.) Seeing yourself in the present where you know what work is yours to do and all that still needs to be transformed. 2.) Seeing yourself from the future, where you see who you are from the perspective of the "you" that you are becoming, the higher 'I'. 3.) Seeing who you have been through your previous life-experiences.

When stepping forward across the threshold into the first degree, the candidate is initially blindfolded. They hear chains rattling, the chains of the fettered and constrained self; distressing and discordant sound rings out from various directions. The pictures in the temple of the first degree are of snakes and demons in the bowels of the earth, and the fires of purification are ready to burn off all that needs to be purified. This purification process of the first degree is a safeguard to the knowledge of the spiritual world; it prevents our subconscious from mingling with the spiritual realities, which it is essential for one to meet just as they are presented.

The small child who has a high fever may even express pictures of these demons, as the fever is working through a purification process of a disease. But the child's consciousness is clearly not in a state of initiation. So it is understood that this purification process is not the true spiritual world, but the training that we are required to pass through in order to clear the way to it, so that we can enter consciously into true spiritual realities. The candidate must endure internal images that would cause the unprepared individual to recoil, and this natural recoiling is an indication of unreadiness. In the ritual of the first degree, we are exposed to great difficulties. But before entering into this initiation and this degree, the candidate is already equipped, as described, which allows them to withstand it.

In the inner world, those who have learned to meditate will at some point be confronted with a bombardment of difficult images testing and trying us while at the same time expressing our own inner world in pictures and images. The candidate only passes through this initiation step after much endurance and internal purification. The development of the "faithful observer" allows them to look upon these images without flinching. The experiencing interior feels every image, and although these images are perceived outside us, it knows that these images are united within us and goes through this purification process. In doing so, the experiencing interior recognizes which images are of its own making, streaming toward it from without but originating from within. This is an essential process because the images of your own making are the doorways to the next realm. The individualized free will must be able to move toward and enter into the images that belong directly to the candidate themselves. Many images will bombard the individual at this stage of the first degree: images of the collective consciousness, images of the environment, which now expresses itself as a vivid image that is sometimes more real than external images, for these images are alive with something. But none of these are doorways. The only doorway to a successful completion of this degree is to be able to penetrate through the images that belong to you. Success is knowing your own shadow.

If someone is induced into this first degree through a consciousness-altering substance, the area they will experience depends on which substance was used to force them there. If it was cannabis, then they may have a sense of bombarding thoughts that are interconnected and yet persistently difficult, as the observer has been induced toward the first degree. If it is through a hallucinogen like ayahuasca, then the thoughts will take on the appearance of the images because the experiencing interior has been induced into the first degree. These are not necessarily contained within the inner perception of the user, but can also manifest as outer hallucinations.

It is understandable that in our industrialized interiority – which has become so dulled, fixed, and hardened – the idea of inducing the observer in a way that allows the user to disengage from the sense world, or the idea of inducing the intensified experiencing interior in a way that liberates one from lifelessness or from being encaged in indoctrination and intellectualism, are becoming more popular. Even for genuine seekers who want to engage in a community working toward spiritual perception, the temptation for induced experiences is increasing. It is said by many that they are attached to the ayahuasca community centered on the music and singing as much as they are to the trip itself; but the substance becomes the vehicle and foundation for the gathering. In this age of deep tearing in the health of our external life together, it is understandable that many are seeking to create change in ways that are radical. However, the spirit is still working with humanity, and we need not give up on the spirit that can still be found in the world through our own capacities and effort. The path of substance use is no substitute.

Cast All Your Votes for Dancing
—Hafiz

I know the voice of depression
Still calls to you.
I know those habits that can ruin your life
Still send their invitation.
But you are with the friend now
And look so much stronger.
You can stay that way
And even bloom.
Keep squeezing drops of sun
From your prayers and work and music
And from your companion's beautiful laughter.
Keep squeezing drops of sun
From the sacred hands and glance of your beloved
And, my dear,
From the most insignificant movements
Of your own holy body.
Learn to recognize the counterfeit coins
That may buy you a moment of pleasure
But then drag you for days
Like a broken man
Behind a farting camel.
You are with the friend now.
Learn what actions of yours delight him
What actions of yours bring freedom
And love.
Whenever you say God's name, dear pilgrim
My ears wish my head was missing
So they could finally kiss each other
And applaud all your nourishing wisdom!
Oh keep squeezing drops of sun

From your prayers and work and music
And from your companions' beautiful laughter
And from the most insignificant movements
Of your own holy body.
Now sweet one,
Be wise
Cast all your votes for dancing.[28]

Some substance users are like a child experiencing a high fever; they have no will available to them with which to penetrate those pictures, or even to detect which pictures are within their own responsibility. If we don't unite with the right doorway through our responsibility toward the images we ourselves have created – though they appear to be outside us – if we don't penetrate through those doorways and we penetrate instead through a different doorway, then we will end up in a different place spiritually and we will not pass the first degree. Instead of entering into the school of love – in which we can begin our education through wisdom and harmony with the knowledge gained in the second degree – we enter into a different schooling.

It would seem an impossibility for any student who has attained a foothold within the second degree to contemplate utilizing consciousness-altering substances at all, or in any way to suggest to another their usefulness on the path. However, individuals who have managed to reverse the effects of the false entry and who have found their way onward to the second degree can always make use of any past experience and indeed be grateful for it. After all, the path has led them to where they are now. But this knowledge holds true for all the events of their past; gratefulness toward past experience is a sign of having a foothold within the second degree if it has been engaged with rightfully and not through diversions.

Rumi, Pay Homage
—Rumi

If God said,

"Rumi, pay homage to everything
that has helped you
enter
my arms,"

there would not be one experience of my life,
not one thought, not one feeling,
not any act, I
would not
bow
to.[29]

One diversion through wrong entry is the mystical schooling of our own grandiosity, although it may not present itself as great and grand. It is the human egotism that gets us here, that holds to a separated life-existence. Love of personal gain, love of the path for personal means, will bring us into this realm of spiritual activity. The industrialized interiority does not know how to be patient and to trust that with committed striving, all that needs to unfold inwardly will indeed unfold at the right time. The wish for intense, quick results is a part of the industrialized state, and these selfish tendencies, these unconscious propellers toward the fast route, make us like beacons attracting the consciousnesses that work to divert humanity. These experiences do not lead to whole self-knowledge, but to self-deception.

These diverting consciousnesses then lead us into further realms of spiritual existence. But we would have no idea of the negativity of these realms because the experiences induced by substance-entry can still produce so-called "peace" or "bliss," and those states are deemed good by our industrialized interiority no matter how they are attained.

This is the path of the unconscious, selfish nature that leads us into our own personal spiritual island and not the united school of love. This is not the only diversion that can result from inducing spiritual experience though substance use. The student may also be diverted into materialistic representations of the sense world, and in this case the activity of the spiritual world appears to manifest with similar forms as those that manifest according to earthly laws and conditions. This has several negative consequences: one being that upon returning to our daily consciousness, we carry back partial pictures from the experience and act as if what was experienced there in the realms of spirit can be lived in the exterior life. For instance, the sense of unifying with the surrounding spiritual world is carried into daily consciousness, bringing misinterpretations to the events of life. Instead of taking life less subjectively, the individual takes it more subjectively, as though the events of life exist for their own self alone. Even their altruistic thoughts and words have a materialistic orientation and an echo of self-service. There are different laws in different realms, and to blend them is to make a mistake in the learning process.

Usually the suggested preparation given to those who are about to take hallucinogens is to be in a good setting because the setting will affect the experience. This is of course true because behind everything manifest in the sense world is a spiritual image of its reality in the spiritual world. If you induce this picturing, then those pictures, along with what you mingle into them, will come to meet you, and what is behind nature and the harmony of nature is very different than what is behind a rave party. Nevertheless, the substance known as MDMA is mostly used in the context of music festivals, as its users are seeking a unity with other people.

The second thing you're instructed to do is to not fight it or you'll have a bad trip – you are advised that you have to surrender to the experience. In the case of induced experience, the overriding of the free individual will is a necessity for the trip. This is counter to the self-developed experience where the free will learns to will, through self-surrender, the entry into other realms; and its recoiling from them would be a sign of unreadiness, a reaction which in this context is purposeful.

It is also asked of many people before taking hallucinogens, "Are you ready to have self-knowledge, are you ready to encounter yourself?" Although this is indeed a part of the experience, it is impossible to know what is being encountered when the experience is being induced by a substance.

But it is clear from the esoteric training that for those who do succeed, without conscious effort, in acquiring something of the first degree, there would need to be some internal strength already available to them. The vast majority of substance users however, are not going to be entering already strengthened, because the strengthening occurs through the initiation training itself.

Substances can only bring the industrialized interiority into a forced relationship to the first degree, the degree of self-knowledge and purification. It can induce the mystical state, belonging to the diverting school of self-interest, but it can't bring us into the training of the wisdom and harmony of the second degree. In order to enter into this wisdom and harmony, the first degree must be managed out of one's own internal resources. Substances cannot produce the strength that is acquired by entering into this degree through your own efforts. The substance can help you enter into it, but it can't get you through it. It is those who get stuck here, and are unable to come into their bodies in the right way afterwards, that face the greatest danger in this present life-experience as a consequence.

If the substance undoes us inwardly, its effects are in opposition to the awakening experience that we may be wanting. Instead of inducing capacities that may help us to learn spiritually, the substance can take away the foundational capacities that we do have – that is, our capacities for attention, attachment, and self-regulation. These foundations are laid in early childhood and contribute greatly to our being able to learn from earthly life. Without them, our journey through the world primarily becomes one of dependence on others for inner stability, just surviving/managing ourselves inwardly, or at best inwardly maintaining the status quo. The most common inner disruption in the earthly world resulting from substance use is that these basic learning and growing capacities begin to diminish.

This in turn has devastating effects on family life and the upbringing of the next generation. If a parent has lost the ability for attention, attachment, and self-regulation, then they cannot provide this ground for the child's development. The fact that in our age many children are born into environments that do not support these three unfolding seeds very well – due to over-stimulation of certain senses, as well as other effects that new technologies are having upon both their environment and upon the inner world of their caregivers – has yet to reveal the full extent of its negative impact on future generations. It is a sign that new inner capacities are needed in order to create the ground of health; for those who are entering into life in this computerized age, the capacities we already have are not resilient enough when faced with the industrialized interiority.

For those who enter the path out of their own efforts, the first degree is still an incredibly challenging test, one in the face of which many turn back because the onslaught can feel overwhelming. If initiation were easy, it would not be the path. "Inner development is a hard path, or it is no path at all." But if one succeeds in entering rightly, one has done so through deep transformation out of one's own efforts, and another step of further transformation awaits.

One must always take into consideration that when the right path is pursued, behind every such experience another immediately arises. If the first experience is there, then the other cannot fail to appear. What one has to bear will immediately be accompanied by the power to really bear it if only one contemplates calmly and takes the time to notice what is seeking to reveal itself in one's soul. If something painful happens, and at the same time a feeling of certainty lives in the soul that there exist forces that can make the pain bearable and with which one can unite oneself, then one will reach the point of relating to such experiences – which would be unbearable if they were to occur in the course of ordinary life – as if one were the observer of oneself in all that one experiences. For this reason, those who are on the path of suprasensory knowledge do inwardly live through the ebb and flow of many waves of feeling and yet show perfect equanimity in their sensory lives.[30]

The inner evolution of the individual is expressed in these rituals of initiation. However, individual evolution is not all that there is, for we have also awakened to collective evolutionary processes. These processes are expressed in the rituals and teachings of the great cosmologies or religions. True initiation only takes place within the individual, for the purpose of entering the heart of God or the divine, or of letting God into our own hearts to form this indissoluble union – this is the true initiation. But outwardly, we can perceive through the corresponding individual initiation experiences that certain teachings, or certain festivals, express the all-encompassing initiation path to the wider world. There are numerous religious festivals that express the initiation path in a form that can work upon the collective interior world of the people of that particular time. Today, because of our industrialized interiority, we are completely losing touch with the esoteric aspect of these rituals, and for many people they have become events based on the empty forms of an old indoctrination that merely amount to time off from work to spend as they wish, but not much more. Or, they may be an expression of a non-individualized, blind belief system handed down to them and lived as an intellectual fact. Both possibilities kill the esoteric life of the outer picture expressed in such festivals.

However, if we take one of the many stories of one of the world religions and look upon it through the light of the symbols it contains, then we may be able to re-enliven it and give meaning to the mystery that is revealed through the story. The story of the Three Kings, seen through the lens of initiation, is one of the stories that contain much value, and those working upon the second degree can begin to read the various world religions in this way. What today seems to be concealed from the dullness of the blunted interior world of the industrialized people, of those who are not yet free from the blind faith of indoctrination and therefore believe their story to be the sole truth, or both, may be revealed for those developing the interior beyond the first degree.

Three Kings' Day is celebrated by some after the twelve days of Christmas, on the 6th of January. This imagination picture describes a dual process: it describes what the individual has to experience, and at the same time it describes a foundational collective change in our evolution as a group. It is said of these three kings that they have walked the royal path. (They are also referred to in external picture as three "wise men"; although, according to the symbolism of the initiation schooling, the word "kings" expresses their degree of initiation.)

It is said that these three kings come from different parts of the world. We have a European named Melchior who brings gold, an Asian named Balthasar who brings frankincense, and an African named Caspar who brings myrrh. These three substances are symbols of the royal striving. Gold is the symbol for seeking God, the divine spiritual world; frankincense is the symbol for cultivating virtue; and myrrh is the symbol of the transformation from mortality to immortality or from transient to eternal being. The three gifts express the knowledge that this is an initiation mystery being revealed.

Symbol, or the law of correspondences, works throughout the ritual world and can only be "read" when the laws of the second degree have been attained through interior development. Someone who has entered the second degree can see the mystery language in the world religions even if the religions of today know nothing of this language. If we are to read this story from the perspective of our earthly life, then, depending on our personal conditioning, the nature of this story changes. In its esoteric picture, it reveals – to those who can read and hear – an evolutionary transformation in the collective consciousness; and at the same time, it produces symbols that those who have achieved entry to the second degree would be able to recognize in their own being, in their path of schooling, even if their own path of training is not related to the tradition that utilizes these symbols.

Also in this story, we hear that the white European, the yellow Asian, and the black African arrive at the red Arabian's birth. These four colors are recognizable and primarily used to indicate the door of the four directions – north, south, east, and west – in many rights and ceremonies. We see them utilized in the sweat lodge ceremonies of the First Peoples of North America, in the cultural life of the Australian first people, and in those traditions in which there was a greater sense of unity between the people, the land, and the elements through a spiritual consciousness of oneness.

But in the age in which this story appears, those who walk the royal path are uniting anew the four directions that must work together for earthly wellbeing and wholeness – not, as before, in the sense of the elements and the land, but now in terms of the races and peoples. These new mysteries are also asking for a future development of working together as human beings. The new element that is contained within the symbol of a king – that is, the newly born child – brings into world evolution a new requirement: the new element of learning to love without selfishness. This is the new prerequisite brought by the new king of the royal path, the internal initiation path.

> Love stands here in the middle and acts as something that must permeate and regulate all of life. It must regulate all of social life. It must also work in a regulating way on the inner impulses we have developed.[31]

From this point on in human development, not only are we seeking God and our relationship to the divine (symbolized by gold), seeking to develop virtues (symbolized by frankincense), and seeking to transform ourselves through immortality (symbolized by myrrh) – but we now have a fourth, new element entering into the initiation mysteries. And that is to seek to develop love: a love that does not contain the selfish element.

This newly born task of inner development is an extraordinary shift for humanity as a whole. It means that initiation may be undertaken by the many because it is no longer just for those capable of developing occult wisdom – the occultists. The kings, who spiritually seek knowledge and power in order to guide others, now have to recognize the path of love. This changes the path of initiation itself. Today, it is expressed that wisdom without love – or power without love – no longer rules as the divine impulse of our age.

This brings to light so many aspects of human life in relationship to the godhead. It suggests that evolution does not belong to humanity alone, but is walked hand in hand with the spiritual world's evolving – and that we have a part to play in that evolution. We are not merely doing the bidding of the spiritual world, but we fully participate in divine planning and creating.

The second degree is already present in the exteriorized ritual – and it is likewise present, in part, even in the experience of the first degree, although is not entered into consciously until the first is fully integrated. Everything in the exteriorized ritual is a symbol for what must be traversed or understood in the interior in order to pass through the second degree. There are seven principles at play in each external ritual: form, strength, number, harmony, word, thought, and 'I'. Each are companions of a spiritual reality, but in the second degree we need to come to understand them in an entirely different light.

Each of these seven principles or steps contains various meanings; and the meanings, when surmounted within, become inner growth. Therefore, individuals uncover the many meanings of each step from out of themselves. However, we can share in some insights that are readily available to the esoteric student through our prior learning of knowledge-based lessons, which help to prepare us for direct experience.

Form is expressed in the external ritual in the fact that it has a certain structure to it. Firstly, there is a form that is followed. This form is quite strict and clear. In the law of correspondences, certain colors, certain signs, and certain symbols are used because they correlate to a conscious activity residing in the spiritual world, and as such are already prescribed. Each participant in the roles of the ritual must "know their lines." We do not make things up; in fact, the script is very clear because it is a part of the form. One expression of the form in the inner world is a recognition that we need a skin, a form, in which to enter rightly into realties that are not perceptible to the senses. The skin is the knowledge, the study, and the preparation, but it primarily forms the container of the individual's consciousness so that the "drop may return to the ocean, but stay in, and aware of, itself." To contemplate form that is formless is a prerequisite for being able to perceive realities beyond the senses.

The strength mentioned here acknowledges the principle in the exteriorized lodge "that the temple is sealed." Sealing the temple means that all those present at the ritual have achieved the degree in question or higher. This is a very important indication of the effects of passing the degree. There is a new strength for the initiate, a strength that we are incapable of developing solely in our relationship to the external world. The strength of being in the united school of love is how we recognize each other: the strength of working together with others in community toward the spirit. The question, "Is the temple sealed?" is also an indication of the vastly different interior experience from one degree to another; one must be ready to enter that level. Once a degree is surmounted, a new degree involving a very different schooling awaits; and the lessons from the past degree now appear useless in their ability to help one pass the new degree, which requires different capacities. It would be like passing a math examination and thinking that the same knowledge that helped one in this can now be utilized to pass a biology examination. Each degree involves a vastly different schooling, as each realm of consciousness has different laws.

Number expresses itself throughout the ritual in the number of times the bell is struck, the hands are clapped, the words are repeated, the words are spoken, and also in the number of participants. Number expresses a new language that is being conveyed, and learning "number law" helps us to understand how number communicates with the depth of the inner world. (In this connection, see *Living Inner Development*.)[32] With numbers, there is a standard of truth that is unarguable. The laws of mathematics are universal facts; for the student of the second degree, certain experiences live inwardly in the same unarguable way.

Harmony is a reflection of the fact that the ritual correlates to a spiritual reality given by the masters of wisdom and harmony. In the interior world, there are four parts of your inner being that are present: thinking, feeling, willing, and the creative master principle, the individual consciousness that must bring all other forces into harmony with each other.

In our age – an age in which we desire autonomy – individuals now want autonomy even over the workings of ritual. In the realm of magic – which is ritualized wisdom being utilized for the manifestations within the sense world – the new term "chaos magic" has arisen. Rather than following through the training of one school, in which each symbol has a specific meaning according to the stream of the training in which one is working, individuals are making up their incantations on the spot, pulling in fragments from various streams. For example: combining a little bit of the Egyptian rites of ritual with something of the Hopi Peoples' prayers, while throwing in the Kabala's naming of things. Today, not only are we trying to personally walk a path that is not meant to be personal, but we are having to come to terms with the fact that many of the older forms of development that are well-recorded, such as traditions of magic, are now different. Even white magic rites of outer manipulation are not utilized in the new mysteries, as the reverse ritual is not about external manifestation and externalized power. The new mysteries reveal the growth away from life in matter and toward an everlasting life in spirit.

The word "laboratory" originally arose from bringing together work and prayer, and the alchemist understands this intimately. What the alchemists are doing is autonomously working outside of a temple ritual, but with all the same ingredients that are used in the temple. They work as individuals working independently through internal development. They too require a deep understanding of the law of correspondences from out of a reliable and concise schooling, and the alchemists' laboratory is the equivalent of the joint external ritual that is now present in order to allow us to learn about internal transformation.

Although freedom is essential to the path, this does not mean the freedom to make things up in the world of the senses. The outer world proves this quite readily. You can decide that you are going to create the color purple by mixing yellow and red, but the experiment proves that it is not possible; it is only possible by mixing blue and red. The world of creating through spiritual activities likewise follows laws and produces definite results, although this must now be perceived inwardly. Making things up more often leads to muddy colors than it does to any clarity and progression; however, we are so hungry for inner experience that we are often more willing to eat fast food than to take the time to learn how to cook from scratch.

In combining streams without knowledge, out of personal desire, we do not know what the results will actually be. Many people make themselves weak, not strong, by such tampering, even though they may have the best of intentions. However, if someone is feeling, as many do, the need to do it their own way and the need to express walking their own path in the world, then this is probably the inner call to their individual task that is speaking in such a deep and inward way.

In the sensory world, at some point there awakens the realization that everyone has something to bring – some capacity that they need to bring into the sensory world around us. This insight awakens our feeling for the collective journey, in which the individual cannot simply live a life in accordance with their own ideals and sense for the meaning of life in seclusion, but in which they must engage in a task that they freely choose, or to which they have been called as though it were given to them. This awareness that "I have something to bring" is a very important opening for an individual working in world evolution.

Through the collective change taking place in our time, very many young people do not know what it is that they have to bring the world. In the age in which heredity held sway, you may well have been born into the very task that you needed to do. You would have known your laboratory, your "work-prayer," not consciously, but through the fact that it was given to you. Not so long ago, by the time people were completing their formal education in school, most had a good idea of what they wanted to do with their lives. Only a few did not know what they wanted to do, and had to seek until their late 20s or early 30s before they could recognize the task that they had to bring.

Today, we're seeing an epidemic of the industrialized interiority, which is being expressed in new generations in such a way that many people really do not have a sense of their own task until much later in life. Contrary to how it was in times past, our current situation is now reversed in the sense that only a very few seem to have clarity about what they want to do with their lives, whereas the vast majority don't get that glimpse until their late 20s or early 30s. But because they are up against an older generation that never had that experience, they feel an anxiousness, as though there is something wrong with them for not having that clarity.

Awakening to one's task is far more individually-determined and conscious today, and it comes far later in one's biography. Once someone does have their task and they know that this is something they are to bring into the world, it changes their relationship to their sense of place and belonging. Those who are secure in their true task in the world are not likely to enter into consciousness-altering substances, because the task brings a type of purpose that engages them with a new level of learning and giving in the world. We would never want to jeopardize the task and realize that the substance actually takes more than it gives. Our task is where we give and also where we learn. It brings deep satisfaction to our sense of progress and it instills images of the second degree that are reflected in the external world – images of wisdom, harmony, and spiritual manifestation.

But, as with all learning, another experience awaits us when we enter into something fully. Once we find our task, our "work prayer," and participate in bringing it into the world, sometimes another awakening occurs. We begin to recognize that what I am bringing in fact has less to do with me than I originally thought. I am a bridge serving to bring the spiritual gifts into the world, and yet I sign my name to its manifestation. We can feel as if we are a fraud or a fake because we know that, in reality, we do not, out of our personal self, produce this, know this, but rather it is a capacity that allows something to come through us – something that is indeed beyond the personal wealth.

When we gain clarity about this to the extent that we know in the depths of our hearts, "of myself, I can do nothing," then the third level of our task arises in which we see that really we are to express the spirit in everything we do.

> Where the spirit does not work with the hand,
> there is no art.
> —Leonardo da Vinci

Following this process, in which we feel that we are bringing the spirit through the hand, we eventually overcome the dualistic view that sees myself over against the spiritual world that is coming through me, and arrive at a state where I myself and the spiritual world are one in the creating.

But because seeking the path from out of a selfish impulse is the hallmark of our industrialized interiority, so few people are willing to really give of themselves, to dedicate themselves to progress, unless there is a guarantee of personal or material wealth and accumulation as a reward.

> The stronger the love one is capable of in the sensory world, the more of that capacity to love will remain with the soul for the suprasensory world.[33]

This quote allows us to understand the bridging relationship that we can bring to the meaning of the signs and symbols we are working with, and to expand our inner knowledge as a preparation for passing the second degree.

The fifth teaching tool of the second degree is called the "word." This indicates the healing nature of the exposure to the harmonious elements of the ritual, as well as the spoken word, which contains a power. These influences help prepare the vessel for this initiation, perhaps more than any other symbol. At the same time, each of these teaching tools is expressed outwardly in the externalized ritual. The meditant is to internally develop the capacities needed to carry these seven activities. And the three higher tools of word, thought, and 'I' require extensive training.

They Can Be Like the Sun
—St. John of the Cross

They can be like the sun, words.

They can do for the heart
what light can
for a field.[34]

So even though we look at the second degree as one degree, it contains many steps, each needing to be explored and integrated. The ritual presents them as working in a harmonious unity. It is not only the word, but the meaning or being of the word that wishes to express itself. What brings the rich and complex understanding of spiritual realms into the ritual is not the thought or the symbol of the thought, but the relationship between the beings that create the signs. The thought is the being's consciousness that is invited to enter the "portals" into the world through the various signs. The 'I' is the tool of completion and the highest of the seven, although they all work together in the outer ritual. The 'I' is not the 'I' of selfness, but rather it is the stage of development in which one human being can, through a spiritual relationship, help another by means of a capacity to grasp the spiritual 'I' that is possessed by all. A path to understanding this 'I' can only be given in an experiential exercise such as the one below.

Contemplate the following:

> In many ways, it is of no consequence for the progress of human life whether it is one oneself who is able to do something or whether it is others who are able to.[35]

When this has been contemplated and taken up inwardly, it becomes the preparation for the next aspect of the exercise, but it is also a purification of any envy or ambition that might exist in the depths of the candidate's heart. It also awakens the understanding that what is important is that a given task is *done*, and not *who* does it. The one who does it then acts out of a free deed, a deed of love.

The second step to this exercise is this: Recall a moment when you had a resolution to perform a deed of love. Now enkindle that moment within you into an intensified experience of love, warmth, and sincerity. This exercise can help us to open the doorway to this highest tool that is performed in the ritual work and contains a reflection of the interior transformation of the meditant.

Those who enact the ritual must do so purely as a deed of love. They must be willing to play the part that any other rightly prepared person could play, because they are ready; the ritual is for the sake of the other's transformation. If in the ritual you imagine that only you could perform this role, then you already show that you have not passed the second degree and are therefore unable to support another's journey through it.

Each degree expresses the victory of the spirit over matter and can be found in all of the world's great festivals. In the Christian festivals, the first degree is reflected in the outer festival of Christmas: the overcoming of the darkness, the victory of light over darkness. The second degree is the victory of love over all that is not love – all that is found in ideology and its practices between birth and death. The third degree, the Easter festival, is the victory of life over death. All three are the victory of the sun-spirit over matter. Light, warmth, and life prevail over ignorance, selfishness, and death.

The third degree allows the initiate to see outside of the sense-bound seeing and live within their eternal skin in the spiritual realms. The strength that arises with the experience of one's eternal life brings to us the ability to be at peace with the world; and, at the same time, we are faced with the trial of whether we still wish to engage with the world's evolving even though we know for ourselves the eternal victory of the immortal nature that has come to consciousness.

This used to be an event for only a very few people in past ages, but it is becoming an event increasingly available and accessible to the many, and not just the chosen few. With each degree that has been surmounted, greater capacities exist to support our fellow human beings in their evolution. In the Masonic lodge, there is a common knowledge of the sign, grip, and word that are expressed as a part of their ritual work. To understand these three in the interior human being helps us to understand the third degree. In the ritual of the third degree, the candidate is pulled out of the tomb of death by the lion's grip of the master. Each individual in the ritual is a representation of aspects of the single human being undergoing interior development. The master is indeed our own higher self. We cannot enter the third degree without the higher 'I' born in spirit and capable of drawing our soul toward its realm. The lion is another symbol for the strength of the heart, the place where the higher 'I' becomes a participant in our interior lives – not as an infrequent intervener in times of need, but as a consistent companion thinking and communicating within this sacred chamber of the heart.

> Just as you have worked upon yourself in the time following the awakening of your consciousness, so you were already working upon yourself before your present consciousness awoke.[36]

We recognize this master who pulls us from the grave as one who has walked with us always, although we were previously unconscious of it. If we are propelled into those higher realms without the necessary preparations and awakenings, without the strength that is gained from surmounting step-by-step all the requirements, then this higher awakening can be a miscarriage that prevents further progress in this incarnation.

Some individuals have recognized this through their substance use – they have recognized that the doors of the inner temple are now permanently closed for the rest of this life. They have "gate-crashed" the first degree enough times to have now been permanently banned. In the sense world, miscarriage brings life to an end, but you can still try again to have a child. In the spiritual world, the miscarriage of the higher 'I' means that you will have to wait for another life to start the possibility of its conscious birth again.

We know that the earth's evolution will not continue forever. Humanity is already seeking out other planets on which we may be able to sustain life, and this industrialized outer world has sped up the death of the earth. The industrialized interiority has made it harder for individuals to develop a living connection to the spiritual world. We think we have time, physically, but we are being told by science that if we do not transform our relationship to the fuel that we use to sustain humanity – transitioning from fossil fuels to green energy (renewables) within the next 50 years – then only two generations from now we will not be able to exist on the planet in the same hospitable state it has offered us until now.

But let's consider this outer picture in an internal way. The earth is slowly becoming like an empty grave from the perspective of the inner world of a part of humanity. At some point in the not so distant future, we will recognize that growth is possible only if it is taken up internally, spiritually. If we are able to recognize this and we have indeed awakened spiritual faculties within us, then the grave of the earth will appear to us as empty, but the spirit has awakened and may continue to live on. For those who are bound solely to this earth, its material gratification, and its material fulfillment, the realization of earth being an empty grave – without any other spiritual awakening – will leave those individuals in a state of empty despair. This will in turn become even more of a battle for the resources of the externalized outer world, destroying it further to wring out of it the drops of life still left.

In the second degree, we have been taught about two distracting forces that wish to divert human progression. It has been revealed to us, and we have been tested in all the ways that are not the path of love. One of those ways is that we are diverted into thinking that the material world is all that exists. It is the individuals trapped in this diversion who will struggle with the dying earth's existence. The other distraction will be the arising of schooling paths that induce spiritual faculties so that the individuals awakened there become spiritual puppets, because they do not stand independently. The new faculties will be induced and not developed out of individual free will, as is required in the next stage of our human development. They will be awakened to themselves but not to a part of world evolution, and therefore they will be unable to truly help others as they will not bear the forces of the universal spiritual 'I'.

The race is on not only for the life of the planet on which we can awaken, but also for the possibility for us to inwardly awaken in such a way that we can have the strength to endure the difficulties that will arise even if we do change to regenerative energy systems and slow down the planet's death process. This is because the internal damage done to the industrialized peoples must still be healed or else they will continue to think, feel, and will in and with their selfish industrialized interiority and thereby continue to produce damaging effects on the inner world of humanity.

There are many individuals who are exposed to this process of the changing times but know nothing about the path of initiation. They have not met an inner schooling and have not yet taken on the path of self-development. However, if they work with the healing principle of love without selfishness, which streams through the unifying connection between all religions and doctrines – if they can work with this love without selfishness, then this brings about the strength that is needed for the development of the individual and the world. The power of love that is now a heritage of our humanness, manifests as a new faculty. The path of initiation is now for all; it is not for the chosen few, but for the many. However, not everyone will walk this path, because it is our free choice to individually step up to the collective call.

The world will still need the occultist's path: those who can have knowledge and wisdom of the future path that the world has yet to awaken to. The world will still need those who have the inner strength and power to move the world forward through outer change. But we need, more than ever before, the middle, the uniting force of love, in order to take humanity to our next phase of life together – a new phase in which we not only think of the joint biosphere outwardly, which we all need to protect and share, but in which we also think of this inward interconnectedness that is ever-present. Knowing that we all play a role in our future, it will be the healing power of unselfish love that awakens our ability to live well together into the future, rather than continue the descent into selfish forms of existence for any one people, race, or nation. This unselfish love is acquired out of ourselves because we are also free not to love. But ask any heart how free it is, and it will speak; abide in it, and you abide in love, and those who abide in love abide in the united life of the divine spiritual world.

> In the temple of the human body is the holy of holies. Most people live in this temple without knowing anything about it. . . . Therein is the holy vessel. . . . One enters the mystery center of one's heart and a divine being arises from this place and unites itself with the divine outside, with the being of the spirit of the world. It is the mission of every single human being and of the whole of humanity to fill themselves with this spirit and to recognize themselves as a center living in this spirit

through which the spiritual light and spiritual warmth can flow into the earth with strength, redeeming it and raising it into spiritual realms.[37]

In the depths of the human heart, we find this center, in which the deepest unity with the spirit is experienced while maintaining full self-awareness. By entering this place often, we grow in our capacity to love and to awaken to a new heart-feeling that loves without selfishness. Here is the holy of holies that we may awaken in order to experience heart-thinking that bridges into the earthly world wisdom without selfish perspectives, and heart-willing that can bridge into our outer world power without any selfish gain. This bridging in the heart is not the same as meeting outside the realms of daily existence by engaging in other realms of spiritual consciousness; this bridging allows us to experience how the love of the spirit is working directly into the world. It allows each person to experience the spirit of love, united in our world, through each individual heart.

Notes

1   See Lisa Romero, *The Inner Work Path* (Mullumbimby, New South Wales: InnerWork Books, 2014), for a foundation and orientation in this approach to meditative practice.

2   Rudolf Steiner, *From the Contents of Esoteric Classes, Recollections of Participants, Part I: 1904–1909*, CW 266 (Berlin, January 29, 1907), accessed on RSArchive.org.

3   Rudolf Steiner, *Knowledge of the Higher Worlds and Its Attainment*, CW 10, trans. Henry B. Monges (Spring Valley, NY: Anthroposophic Press, 1947), Chapter IX: "The Splitting of the Human Personality during Spiritual Training."

4   George E. Vaillant, *Triumphs of Experience: The Men of the Harvard Grant Study* (Cambridge, MA: Belknap Press, Reprint edition, 2015).

5   Rudolf Steiner, *Knowledge of the Higher Worlds*, Chapter II: "The Stages of Initiation," Section: "The Control of Thoughts and Feelings." This passage revised by T. O'Keefe.

6   Rudolf Steiner, *Knowledge of the Higher Worlds*, Chapter IX.

7   Rudolf Steiner, *Meditations for Harmony and Healing: Finding the Greater Self*, trans. Matthew Barton (Forest Row, UK: Rudolf Steiner Press, 2018), p. 49.

8   Martin Luther King Jr.; from a lecture at the University of Michigan, Hill Auditorium, November 5, 1962 (Bentley Historical Library).

9   Owen Barfield, *Worlds Apart* (Oxford, UK: Barfield Press UK, 2010).

10 See Owen Barfield's official website, where this is the main quotation: OwenBarfield.org.

11 Lisa Romero, *Spirit-Led Community: Healing the Impact of Technology* (Mullumbimby, New South Wales: InnerWork Books, 2018).

12   Rudolf Steiner, *A Path to Self-Knowledge: In Eight Medita-tions*, CW 16, trans. J. Selg and T. O'Keefe (New York, NY: Chadwick Library Edition, forthcoming in 2019), pp. 81–82.

13   Ed. Daniel Ladinsky, *Love Poems from God: Twelve Sacred Voices from the East and West* (New York, NY: Penguin Books, 2002), p. 31.

14   Rudolf Steiner, *Mantric Sayings: Meditations, 1903–1925*, CW 268 (Great Barrington, MA: SteinerBooks, 2015).

15   Rudolf Steiner, *Freemasonry and Ritual Work*, CW 265 (Great Barrington, MA: SteinerBooks, 2007). From the lesson on the Human Being's Mission on Earth, p. 429 (translation adapted).

16   Rudolf Steiner, *Mantric Sayings*, p. 151.

17   Ed. Daniel Ladinsky, *Love Poems from God*, p. 170.

18   Rudolf Steiner, *Knowledge of the Higher Worlds*, Chapter V: "The Conditions of Esoteric Training" (translation adapted).

19   Ibid.

20   Ibid.

21   Ibid.

22   Ibid.

23   Ibid.

24   Ibid.

25   Séamus O. Maynard.

26   Lisa Romero, *Living Inner Development: The Necessity of True Inner Development in the Light of Anthroposophy* (Mullumbimby, New South Wales: InnerWork Books,, 2016).

27   Rudolf Steiner, *The Temple Legend*, CW 93 (Forest Row, UK: Rudolf Steiner Press, 1997).

28   Rudolf Steiner, *A Path to Self-Knowledge*, pp. 84–85.

29   Hafiz, *I Heard God Laughing: Poems of Hope and Joy* (New York, NY: Penguin Books, 2006), trans. Daniel Ladinsky.

30   Ed. Daniel Ladinsky, *Love Poems from God*, p. 68.

31   Rudolf Steiner, *A Path to Self-Knowledge*, pp. 81–82.

32   Rudolf Steiner, *The Spiritual Foundation of Morality: Francis of Assisi and the Christ Impulse* (Hudson, NY: Anthroposophic Press, 1995).

33   Lisa Romero, *Living Inner Development*.

34   Rudolf Steiner, *A Path to Self-Knowledge*, p. 65.

35   Ed. Daniel Ladinsky, *Love Poems from God*, p. 324.

36   Rudolf Steiner, *A Path to Self-Knowledge*, p. 76 (translation adapted). The full passage is as follows: "An intense and repeated (meditative) 'living together with' the thought that, in many ways, it is of no consequence for the course of human life whether it is one oneself who is able to do something or whether it is others who are able to, can bring one a long way toward genuine equanimity regarding what one feels as one's innermost destiny."

37   Rudolf Steiner, *A Path to Self-Knowledge*, p. 78. The full passage is as follows: "Then one can bring oneself to the point of saying to oneself: 'Just as you have worked upon yourself in the time following the awakening of your consciousness, so you were already working upon yourself before your present consciousness awoke.'"

38   Rudolf Steiner, *Freemasonry and Ritual Work*, p. 429 (translation adapted).

About the Author

LISA ROMERO is the author of several books on inner development, as well as a complementary health practitioner and an adult educator who has been offering healthcare and education enriched by anthroposophy since 1993. From 2006, the primary focus of her work has been on teaching inner development and anthroposophic meditation.

Her six books are *The Inner Work Path: A Foundation for Meditative Practice in the Light of Anthroposophy* (2014); *Developing the Self – Through the Inner Work Path in the Light of Anthroposophy* (2015); *Living Inner Development: The Necessity of True Inner Development in the Light of Anthroposophy* (2016); *Sex Education and the Spirit: Understanding Our Communal Responsibility for the Healthy Development of Gender and Sexuality within Society* (2017); *Spirit-led Community: Healing the Impact of Technology* (2018); and *A Bridge to Spirit: Understanding Conscious Self Development and Consciousness-Altering Substances* (2019).

Through the Inner Work Path, Lisa offers lectures, courses, and retreats for personal and professional development in communities and schools worldwide. Lisa's capacity to deliver esoteric wisdom with insight and understanding allows her to meet the diverse needs of communities and professions.

For many years, Lisa lectured on health and nutrition and male/female studies at Sydney Rudolf Steiner College, where she continues to give lectures on inner development to the tutors.

Since 1999, she has been presenting on the subject of gender, sexuality, and spiritual life. She has been working with Waldorf schools as a part of their "health and wellbeing" curriculum, working directly with the students, teachers, and parents on this theme. Lisa has contributed to and is an adviser for the "Health and Personal Development for the Australian Steiner Curriculum Framework." She has developed training courses and facilitates professional development on this subject for teachers and health professionals.

Lisa designed and facilitated EduCareDo "Towards Health and Healing," which has offered eight-year courses focused on working with therapists from all modalities, as well as with Waldorf teachers toward cultivating the depth of anthroposophic insight through practical applications of therapeutic and pedagogical methods.

Lisa Romero is a tutor, contributor, and director of Inner Work Path, EduCareDo, Developing the Self – Developing the World, and the Y Project. EduCareDo offers self-directed, distance-learning courses based on the principal ideas of Rudolf Steiner. Developing the Self – Developing the World offers community education, and the Y Project supports the transition of young people into healthy community life.

For meditation courses and talks,
visit innerworkpath.com

For more information on school and community education,
visit developingtheself.org

For distance learning courses in anthroposophy,
visit educaredo.org